The UPWARD CALL

The UPWARD CALL

Spiritual Formation and the Holy Life

WESLEY D. TRACY
E. DEE FREEBORN
JANINE TARTAGLIA
MORRIS A. WEIGELT

Beacon Hill Press of Kansas City
Kansas City, Missouri

Copyright 1994
by Beacon Hill Press of Kansas City

ISBN: 083-411-5166

Continuing Lay Training Unit 115.13B

Printed in the United States of America

Cover Design: Paul Franitza

10   9   8   7   6   5   4   3   2   1

CONTENTS

PART IV
FINDING WAYS TO SERVE OTHERS
ON OUR JOURNEY

The Upward Call

Not that I have already attained,
or am already perfected;
but I press on,
that I may lay hold of that for which Christ Jesus
has also laid hold of me.
Brethren, I do not count myself to have apprehended;
but one thing I do,
forgetting those things which are behind
and reaching forward
to those things which are ahead,
I press toward the goal
for the prize of the
upward call of God in Christ Jesus.

PHIL. 3:12-14, NJKV

PREFACE

This book is about a marriage—a marriage between spiritual formation and the Wesleyan teaching of holiness. They have so much in common that a marriage is in order. Their compatibility centers in their mutual concern for holy living. For both, the standard is Christlikeness. There can be no other meaningful measurement for spiritual formation or sanctified living.

Wesleyan spirituality boldly proclaims that holiness of heart and life is available for every believer by way of sanctifying grace. Wesleyan spirituality clearly shows the believer the way to the highway of holiness. The method of Wesleyan discipleship is very effective, too, within and beyond its own borders.

In *The Classics of Western Spirituality*, Frank Whaling wrote, "It is not so much that [Wesleyan] spirituality has been tried and found wanting. Certain elements of it have been tried and have borne fruit especially through the medium of the Methodist tradition. Even so, in its wholeness, the spirituality of the Wesleys has never been fully tried."[1]

The essence of the Wesleyan doctrine of holiness has to do with the restoration of the image of God in humanity expressed in *Christlikeness,* and the goal of spiritual formation is to bring the believer to such Christlikeness that it is appropriate to speak of Christ being formed in the believer's heart. This tradition is 2,000 years old, or at least as old as Paul's letter to the Galatians in which he wrote: "My little children, with whom I am again in travail *until Christ be formed in you!*" (Gal. 4:19, RSV, emphasis added).

The basic core of spiritual formation is an enabling relationship with God based upon grace alone. Spiritual formation occurs through a dynamic, growing relationship with God. The only norm or standard for measuring spiritual formation is *Christlikeness.*

Thus, these two, the Wesleyan doctrine of holiness and the teachings of the spiritual formation tradition, come now to be joined in holy matrimony on the pages of this book—at least that is the aim. It is hoped this book will help people answer the upward call of God in Christ, find the path to spiritual life, and persevere on the highway of holiness.

The authors of this book have studied a vast body of literature on spirituality. We have probed major works from every Christian century and almost every Christian generation. Dr. Weigelt and Dr. Freeborn teach spiritual formation at Nazarene Theological Seminary, in local churches, and at district retreats and conferences. Dr. Tracy is a specialist in Wesleyan spiritual theology. He has written, taught, and preached widely on this subject. Janine Tartaglia is a vigorous and successful minister of the gospel, a noted speaker, a devoted Christian. She brings a feminine approach to the task, along with her valuable experience in broadcast journalism and mass media communication.

Dr. Weigelt is primarily responsible for chaps. 1—5 and 10. Dr. Freeborn was the primary writer of chaps. 6—9. Janine Tartaglia wrote the last three chapters of the book. Dr. Tracy served as the leader of the writing team, editing the manuscript, and writing chaps. 11—16. We tell you this so that when the authors use the first person in relating a personal experience, you can find out (if you care to) whose experience it was.

The pattern of the book presents the holy life as a journey—as indeed it is. **Part I, Finding the Path,** takes the reader through the beginning of the journey. Grace is the beginning—*atoning grace* is brought about by the "Lamb slain from the foundation of the world" (Rev. 13:8, KJV); prevenient or preventing grace is that whereby every sinner is given the power to choose God and good when he or she hears "the upward call."

We stress saving grace because, without clear Christian conversion, there is no possibility for spiritual formation. Sanctifying grace, one of the most precious jewels in the Wesleyan heritage, makes new dimensions of Christlikeness possible. Apart from grace, there can be no spiritual formation or holy living. Apart from grace, the spiritual disciplines, however faithfully practiced, turn out to be the pathetic rags of self-righteousness.

Part II, Finding Resources for the Journey, explores the fundamental spiritual disciplines. We look at the foundational means of grace. Recognizing the creative and sustaining role of grace at every stage in the journey, we see the disciplines are the means by which grace flows into our lives for personal spiritual growth. Yet the focus remains on our relationship with God because the disciplines only provide the context in which grace is likely to function. We will present prayer, meditation, Bible study, spiritual reading, blessed subtractions, and journaling as avenues of grace. We will also explore what all this means in light of personality differences.

Part III, Finding Companions on the Way, teaches us that the holy life is a community affair. Christians in churches, classes, small groups, families, and in the roles of spiritual friends and faith mentors help each other on the highway of holiness.

This is not a frill; it is a requirement. Whatever else the Church is, it is a called-out *community*. A solitary Christian is a contradiction in terms, an oxymoron, if you please. John Wesley was right when he taught us that if we do not have spiritual companions on the way to the New Jerusalem, we must make them—for no one can travel that journey alone.

Part IV, Finding Ways to Serve Others on Our Journey, discusses self-sacrificing Christian service as a spiritual discipline necessary to the holy life. A spirituality that does not result in self-giving service is a farce. If you have the heart of Christ, you will reach out to your family, your church, and your community with the hands of Christ.

Study of the Scriptures is a vital part of every chapter of this book. Faithful attention to the "For Personal Reflection and Action" section at the end of each chapter will bring the reader into vital contact with several of the Epistles of Paul. The principal books for study are Galatians, Ephesians, Philippians, and 1 Thessalonians. The leader's guide, published under separate cover, also stresses Bible study.

Every Christian generation has produced two kinds of Christians: the common, ordinary garden variety, and those who have discovered the deeper life. Some call this deeper life entire sanctification. Others call it the baptism with the Spirit, Christian perfection, perfect love, or holiness of heart and life. Whatever the label, it reflects a deeper experience of Christlikeness.

Many Christians today hear the upward call of God to holiness. But they do not know how to answer the call. In a moment of inspiration they hear the still, small voice and catch a glimpse of a land filled with rare spiritual vistas. They treasure the vision and sense a deep hunger of the soul for more of God. But in the "maddening maze of things"—such as car pools, night classes, music lessons, soccer practice, and church committee meetings, the vision fades and on they go, stumbling along the Mediocre Way instead of the Highway of Holiness.

It is hoped this book will help you respond to the hunger in your soul, to the upward call of God to a holy life of growing Christlikeness.

Here is our definition of spiritual formation. Let it be a road map as you study this book.

The whole person in relationship with God, within the community of believers, growing in Christlikeness, reflected in a Spirit-directed, disciplined lifestyle, and demonstrated in redemptive action in our world.

12

PART I

Finding the Path

The whole person in relationship with God . . .

◆

**Until we stop running away from ourselves
and hiding from God, there is no real possibility
of spiritual growth.**

◆

**But the Lord God called to the man, and said to him,
"Where are you?"**
(Gen. 3:9, RSV).

◆

**Come to me, all you who are weary and burdened,
and I will give you rest**
(Matt. 11:28, NIV).
—Jesus of Nazareth

Introduction to Part I

GETTING "UNLOST"

Have you ever been really lost—so lost that you had absolutely no clue about how to find your way back—so lost that fear began to paralyze you into total inactivity?

Such emotions are even more terrorizing when they relate to spiritual lostness. As a result, we may develop elaborate avoidance techniques so that we stop thinking about it and stop feeling those paralyzing feelings.

When we are lost, we often long for a parental set of hands to come and twirl us about until we are facing in the right direction. The security of having someone direct us back at least to the starting point of the journey would be an enormous relief.

In Part I of this book the aim is to bring you back again to the starting point of things spiritual. We hope to help you become "unlost." We hope you will be found by the truth and direction of God's Word. We hope you will find release from the anxieties that lostness brings.

Augustine spoke for all of us in this classic line: "The heart is restless until it finds its rest in Thee." Modern paraphrases suggest that there is a God-shaped vacuum at the core of our personhood that can be satisfied only with a dynamic relationship with the Creator.

Many voices promise freedom and release from stress and potential for development. But many such security brokers and self-help prophets pay no attention to the Scriptures and do not know the Lord.

We would like to invite you to consider the Wesleyan way to spiritual development. We invite you to allow the Word of God to help you find the authentic starting point. Allow yourself to be captivated by God. The apostle Paul wrote: "But now that you have come to know God, or rather to be known by God" (Gal. 4:9, RSV).

In the Bible we are introduced to the God who is seeking a relationship with us. Even though sin has sharply curtailed the possibilities of such a dynamic relationship, Paul reminds us: "But where sin increased, grace abounded all the more" (Rom. 5:20). The radical optimism of grace in the New Testament is our invitation to spiritual growth —to a relationship with the God of the universe.

We pray that you will find the path!

We pray that you will get "unlost"!

We pray that you will overcome your restlessness and fear and discover the freedom of holy living.

Spiritual development is not a matter of
self-achievement, self-help, or self-discipline. It is
strictly a matter of *relationship* with God.

1

Walking with God

The crisp and crackly Dakota winter night sent me shivering to my room, but not to sleep. I dragged my bed to the northern window and propped myself up on a pillow to watch God's cosmic light show—the aurora borealis. I was only 12 years old, and the northern lights spectacular created an inexpressible amazement

The lights shifted in a moving array of colors. There were reds and blues and oranges and greens and yellows and every combination of color in between. For a number of hours those lights pulsed and shifted in a kaleidoscope of color. What a light show!

I was deeply moved by the immensity of the universe and the smallness of the boy observing that vast display of color and power. Although I was unable to frame the concept, God was introducing me to the central principle of spiritual formation. **There is no possibility of spiritual formation apart from "intersections" or encounters with God.** That is to say, spiritual development is not a matter of self-achievement, self-help, or self-discipline. It is strictly a matter of *relationship* with God.

To discuss spiritual formation as an end in itself, or as

a prescription for reducing stress, or as a route to psychological wholeness, is to miss the primary point. At the heart of spiritual development is a carefully nurtured relationship with God.

GOD'S CALL TO RELATIONSHIP ECHOES THROUGHOUT THE OLD TESTAMENT

Study the Old Testament and you discover a seeking God. God wanders through its sacred histories, inviting mere mortals to relationship. His voice echoes through the corridors of those ancient centuries, calling the lost, the bruised, the sin-sick, even the defiant rebels to redeeming relationship with the God of all the earth.

1. God Calls in the Cool of the Evening

The call of God to relationship comes first to Adam and Eve in the garden. "They heard the sound of the Lord God walking in the garden at the time of the evening breeze" (Gen. 3:8). After they sinned and began hiding from God, the haunting call, "Adam, where are you?" was sounded for the first time. God has continued calling for His children down through the ages.

2. God Invites Three Guys to Go for a Walk —a Long Walk

The covenant call of God to Abram was an invitation to walk in fellowship with God: "I am God Almighty; walk before me, and be blameless" (Gen. 17:1). Enoch and Noah were also called to "walk" with God. Indeed, the spiritual life is a walk, a lifelong journey, an upward call to walk the highway of holiness in fellowship with God.

God repeatedly calls persons and Israel to relationship. Often that relationship is described as walking together. Sometimes it is compared to a father-son or marriage relationship. Any violation of that relationship is a gross infidelity that sabotages spiritual development.

3. A Daily Wake-Up Call from God

The people of Israel were to say the Shema daily:

"Hear, O Israel: The Lord our God is one Lord; and you shall love the Lord your God with all your heart, and with all your soul, and with all your might. And these words which I command you this day shall be upon your heart" (Deut. 6:4-6, RSV). Thus, every day they reminded themselves of the importance of a relationship with God.

4. God Calls a Man Named Deceiver

Let's look at the "intersection" Jacob had with God as recorded in Genesis 28. With his mother's help, Jacob—known as the deceiver—had cheated his brother, Esau, out of the blessing reserved for the firstborn son. The grudge that Esau now held against Jacob was so bitter that his mother sent him out of the country.

On the lam and filled with guilt, Jacob ran into God, who intervened to reaffirm the covenant He had originally made with his grandfather, Abraham. Jacob's own words keep echoing in our hearts: "Surely the Lord is in this place—and I did not know it! . . . How awesome is this place! This is none other than the house of God, and this is the gate of heaven" (Gen. 28:16-17).

To become aware of God's careful shepherding of our lives—even when we are attempting to escape—teaches us the foundational truth of spiritual formation. God is always seeking relationship.

5. God Calls a Nation that Forgot Fidelity

I have been deeply influenced by the record of the appearance of God to Moses as recorded in the 33rd chapter of Exodus. After receiving the Ten Commandments from God at Mount Sinai, Moses returned to the foot of the mountain and found the people cavorting around the golden calf. Moses fell to his knees to intercede with God for his people. Listen to his prayer: "If your Presence does not go with us, do not send us up from here. How will anyone know that you are pleased with me and with your people unless you go with us? What else will distinguish me and your people from all the other people on the face of the earth?" (Exod. 33:15-16, NIV).

Moses kept on pressing until God promised to demonstrate His presence. He hid Moses in the cleft of the rock and covered him with His hand while His divine glory passed. Then God removed His hand and Moses was able to see God as He walked on by. God gave Moses the second edition of the Ten Commandments, and he was sent back to his people. The tablets of the law were, and are, a guide to relating to others and to God himself. God was calling His people back into redemptive relationship.

> **Indeed, the spiritual life is a walk,
> a lifelong journey, an upward call
> to walk the highway of holiness
> in fellowship with God.**

Genuine spiritual formation can begin only with a saving encounter with God. God is out to intersect your path, to offer you a redemptive relationship. Have you noticed you keep bumping into Him at every corner?

6. God Calls Through the Tears of a Preacher

God spoke through Jeremiah to call a rebellious people back to redemptive relationship. Israel had violated God's law repeatedly. Jeremiah understood that God's mercy does not mean that the consequences of sin will not occur. He stressed the certainty of the punishment that Israel had brought upon herself.

Jeremiah is known as the weeping prophet. But he is also the prophet of return. His weeping voice called Israel to repent and return. "Make yourself guideposts; consider well the highway, the road by which you went. Return, O virgin Israel, return to these your cities" (31:21, RSV).

7. God Has Many Voices

The Old Testament is filled with records of God's strategic "intersections" or encounters with His people. Sometimes He comes in rebuke and condemnation. Sometimes He comes in concern and care. Sometimes He comes in a night vision. Sometimes He comes through His chosen prophets. Sometimes He comes through the fire and the whirlwind. Sometimes He comes in the still, small voice. But the record shouts clearly that He always comes. God is the initiator of relationship. The concept of a seeking God is a cornerstone of both Wesleyan and biblical spirituality. Without those special "intersections" with God, we will never find saving and sanctifying grace, and our deepest needs will go unmet.

GOD'S CALL TO RELATIONSHIP
REECHOES IN THE NEW TESTAMENT

The understanding of this primary principle of spiritual formation is sharpened when we turn to the New Testament.

1. The Fulfillment of the Law

When the lawyer asks Jesus to identify the central point of the law, Jesus focuses on a loving relationship with God: "You shall love the Lord your God with all your heart, and with all your soul, and with all your mind. This is the great and first commandment" (Matt. 22:37-38, RSV).

2. God Speaks in Christ

The writer to the Hebrews tells us that the God who spoke in diverse ways and different places through the prophets has now spoken definitively in Jesus Christ. It is this Christ who says: "No one knows the Father except the Son and any one to whom the Son chooses to reveal him. Come to me, all who labor and are heavy laden, and I will give you rest. Take my yoke upon you, and learn from me; for I am gentle and lowly in heart, and you will find rest for your souls. For my yoke is easy, and my burden is light" (Matt. 11:27-30, RSV).

3. The Parables Picture a Seeking God

The parables of our Lord vividly underline the seeking aspect of God. The parables of the lost sheep, the lost coin, and the lost son in Luke 15, for example, emphasize not only the seeking/searching aspect of the Heavenly Father's love but also the joy over the recovery of the lost. Each of these parables ends with the same refrain—celebration at recovery.

4. Jesus Was a Flesh-and-blood Invitation to Fellowship with God

The model of Jesus himself points in the same direction. From the moment of His inaugural sermon, recorded in Luke 4, it is clear that redemption, recovery, and relationship are primary themes of His life and ministry. He reaches out to the outcast, the disenfranchised, the poor, the maimed, and the blind. His love is a reflection of the Father's love.

> **God is searching for you to offer you a redemptive relationship. That's why you keep bumping into Him at every corner!**

The model of Jesus' own life reinforces the principle. His prayer life points in the same direction. He taught His disciples to pray, beginning with "Abba, Father." His prayer in the garden, according to John 17, was one of intimacy and familiarity. He acknowledges that He and the Father are one and prays that the same relationship will characterize His disciples.

The repeated emphasis upon forgiveness in sermon and parable reinforces the awareness that spirituality begins and ends in a relationship with God. The Lord's Prayer makes forgiveness one of the central petitions. The death of Christ becomes the setting in which He models forgiveness by extending it to those who have crucified Him.

5. The Crucifixion Pleads, "Look— I Love You This Much"

John 3:16-17, memorized by nearly everyone reading

this book, captures this theme: "For God so loved the world that he gave his only Son, that whoever believes in him should not perish but have eternal life. For God sent the Son into the world, not to condemn the world, but that the world might be saved through him" (RSV).

The death of Jesus on the Cross becomes the ultimate evidence that relationship with God is at the heart of Christianity. He died that we might be forgiven and enjoy eternal life—which is defined by John as knowing God (John 17:3).

▶ For Personal Reflection and Action ◀

So What Do You Expect Me to Do About This?

Expect is a bossy sort of word. Rather, let me simply invite you to do the following.

1. Realize That Holy Living and Spiritual Formation Are Gifts from God

The fulfillment of your heart's hunger will not be found in more rigid self-discipline, a better education, resolve to turn over a new leaf, a glitzy self-help book complete with cassette tapes, a love affair, or even in a pay raise. To seek to fill the God-shaped hunger in your heart with such futility is to live out the scene in a John Updike novel, where a despairing worker sits down on a crate of self-help books to plot his suicide. Encounters, or "intersections," with God that lead to relationship with Him are our only hope for spiritual growth, holiness, and happiness.

2. Reflect on Past "Intersections" with God

With amazing regularity, He has been intersecting your life. Even if you have been running away, like Jacob or Jonah, He has found you—has He not? Give yourself time to ponder those sacred experiences. Make a list of five of the most significant intersections with God in the course of your life. Include those moments when it became apparent only in retrospect that God had touched you.

3. Renew Your Commitment to Nurture the Relationship to Which God Calls You

Respond to God's call with faith and obedience, with careful nurturing of that relationship in submissive and grateful love to the one who has come to us in Christ.

All relationships require careful nurture. Friendships that are not nurtured deteriorate and die. Marriages that are not carefully nurtured develop emotional distances too great to overcome. Your relationship with God is too precious to waste or risk. Listen for His still, small voice. He is at your heart's door even at this moment.

4. Review the Problem of Sin

The hope for holy living and a growing relationship with God has been severely contaminated by sin. In the next chapter we shall explore the ways in which sin sabotages spiritual formation and holy living. Read it carefully and soon.

5. Bible Study

Read the following passages, noting the theme of a loving God reaching out to bring sinners into a redeeming relationship:

Gal. 3:1—4:7 (especially 3:24-29 and 4:4-7)

Eph. 2:1-21

Phil. 2:5-11

As you contemplate these scriptures and the "calling God" pictured in this chapter, make this hymn part of your devotions: "Give Me Thy Heart" (Hymn 332 in *Sing to the Lord,* Lillenas Publishing Co., 1993).

> Christian conversion is not a case of fanning that
> little spiritual spark in the human soul into a flame.
> It is a case of invading a dark and doomed soul
> with spiritual light from above.
>
> —Steve Turner
> "Lean, Green, and Meaningless"

2

Sabotaged by Sin

In *Scandalous Risks*, Susan Howatch tells the compelling story of Venetia Flaxton, a young woman who falls in love with a friend of the family, who happens to be a clergyman—in fact, the dean of the cathedral. They develop a secret love affair and rationalize their behavior.

Doubts begin to paralyze the mind of the young woman. She goes one day to seek counsel from an elderly priest. Venetia justifies the violation of ethical and moral rules by arguing that the metaphorical language of past generations no longer adequately describes God. Love is all the explanation one needs.

The priest turns to a contemporary analogy to describe what is happening to Venetia. When the atomic bomb was dropped on Hiroshima, many were killed outright. Some appeared to be unscathed on the basis of external observation, but "they had been contaminated by a great pollutant. It was invisible, but it entered the flesh of those unfortunate victims and settled in their bones and is to this very day busy destroying them."[1] He spells out the insidious way in which everything is contaminated by sin.

Near the end of the novel, Venetia finally admits the damage is so serious that she can no longer find God.

THE FRUSTRATION OF GOD'S DESIGN

This example from a contemporary novel underlines a second major principle of spiritual formation: **Spiritual formation must recognize that God's design has been seriously frustrated by sin.** The resultant contamination has forever affected the way in which we approach God.

Many who write and speak in the field of spiritual development give no evidence that they are aware of the devastating consequences of sin. They imply that effort and appropriate conditions will produce spiritual formation. It is necessary only to move relatively smoothly up the sequence from *unholy* to *holy*.

Words like *spiritual* and *spiritual potential* are creeping into some of the strangest contexts. Steve Turner wrote: "As used in secular discourse, *spiritual* can refer to anything that cannot either be tested in a laboratory or bolted to the floor."[2] When *spiritual* is defined without recognition of sin, destructive confusion results.

> Christian conversion is not a case of fanning that little spiritual spark in the human soul into a flame. It is a case of invading a dark and doomed soul with spiritual light from above . . . The evidence that Saint Paul had passed from spiritual death to spiritual life was not that he heard a voice, saw a light, and temporarily lost his sight, but that love replaced his hatred, that patience replaced his testiness, and that meekness replaced his pride.[3]

The light of the Word is our only guide. The Bible's recognition of the destructiveness of sin will enable us to understand the essential elements in spiritual development.

1. A Contaminated Relationship with God

The Bible begins with God's creative work. The picture of God bending down and breathing the breath of life into that first person is simply beautiful. The very next chapter rehearses the drastic results of broken relationship. Sin immediately contaminated everything.

We understand contamination. Oil spills and chemical dumping create irreversible damage. The disposal of nuclear waste has become a major problem. Radioactive accidents, such as the one at Chernobyl, have endangered or destroyed countless lives. Even more devastating is the contamination of life by the power of sin. Sin is a lethal cancer that sabotages spiritual formation and holiness. Its contamination floods the spiritual environment. Walter Brueggemann wrote: "The poison of guilt is at least as dangerous as nuclear waste. It must be put away where it cannot destroy or contaminate."[4]

| **Sin is a lethal cancer that sabotages spiritual formation.** |

Ray Dunning, in *Grace, Faith, and Holiness,* states that the image of God in human beings included four primary and essential freedoms: freedom for God, freedom for the other, freedom from the earth or the world, and freedom from self-domination.[5] All these freedoms were lost at the Fall.

In his sermon "The New Birth" John Wesley described the results of the Fall:

> He lost the life of God: he was separated from Him, in union with whom his spiritual life consisted . . . the love of God was extinguished in his soul . . . so had he lost both the knowledge and love of God, without which the image of God could not subsist of this, therefore, he was deprived . . . and became unholy as well as unhappy. In the room of this he sunk into pride and self-will, the very image of the devil; and into sensual appetites and desires, the image of the beasts.[6]

2. **The Inability to Trust God**

The essence of sin, then, is a refusal to trust God—an

exaltation of self to the exclusion of God with a resultant disobedience. Thus, spiritual formation is sabotaged from the beginning.

The secretive way in which sin entraps, deceives, and destroys creates a maze of difficulties. The sin problem started in the garden of Eden with the deception of Adam by Eve. They both began to doubt God and went into hiding. They were ashamed and were unable to face God. So the rich and dynamic relationship they previously enjoyed with God was disrupted.

Broken relationships with God mess up relationships with other persons. It was not long after the exclusion from the garden that murder entered the picture—Cain killed Abel. Family breakup is clearly illustrated in the remainder of Genesis. Israel, as the people of God, struggle in their relationship between God and His people who cannot trust the Lord.

3. God Is Serious—Dead Serious—About Sin

One example from the checkered history of Israel will exhibit the seriousness with which God views sin.

The setting is the Book of Numbers. The Hebrews stood at the southern entrance to the land of promise, according to chap. 13. Spies had already checked out the land. The majority report said the opposition was too formidable. Only two of the spies recommended trusting God to aid them.

As rebellion began among the people, Moses and Aaron fell facedown in front of the whole assembly. Joshua warned the people tersely: "Only, do not rebel against the Lord" (Num. 14:9).

After some special pleading, Moses convinced the Lord that wiping out the whole nation at one blow would be poor public relations as far as Egypt was concerned. But listen to the consequences: "Then the Lord said, 'I have pardoned, according to your word; but truly, as I live, and as all the earth shall be filled with the glory of the Lord, none of the men who have seen my glory and my signs which I wrought in Egypt and in the wilderness, and yet have put me to the proof these ten times and have not hearkened to my voice, shall see the land which I swore to give to their fathers; and *none of those who despised me* shall see it'" (Num. 14:20-23, RSV, emphasis added).

The Psalmist understood that God is serious—dead serious—when He views such rebellion. "For forty years I loathed that generation and said, 'They are a people who err in heart, and they do not regard my ways.' Therefore I swore in my anger that they should not enter my rest" (Ps. 95:10-11, RSV).

> **One of the most deceitful aspects of sinfulness is the temptation to disguise the true understanding of sin for our own purposes.**

When you check the final phrase in the original language, you find only an "if" clause, without the rest of the sentence. The Hebrew and the Greek both read: "If they ever enter my rest . . ."! And it is clear that God means business. The consequences are not spelled out, but you don't need a fifth grade education to figure out that no one is exempt. Those words of finality of Num. 14:23 still shout across the centuries: "No one who has treated me with contempt will ever see it" (NIV).

THE NEW TESTAMENT FURTHER DEFINES THIS DEVASTATION

The New Testament continues the same theme. The sabotaging effects of sin have overshadowed every aspect of life. The effects of Adam's sin are summarized in Rom. 5:12-14: "Therefore as sin came into the world through one man and death through sin, and so death spread to all men because all men sinned—sin indeed was in the world before the law was given, but sin is not counted where there is no law. Yet death reigned from Adam to Moses, even over those whose sins were not like the transgression of Adam, who was a type of the one who was to come" (RSV). Only the gracious gift of God's beloved Son is able to resolve the issue.

1. Sin Has a Thousand Faces

In the early chapters of Romans, Paul describes the pervasiveness of the sin. It breaks out in many different forms. God's growing frustration climaxes in the announcement that human beings are released to wallow in their own filth. The crescendo of sinfulness is summarized in 1:29-31: "They were filled with all manner of wickedness, evil, covetousness, malice. Full of envy, murder, strife, deceit, malignity, they are gossips, slanderers, haters of God, insolent, haughty, boastful, inventors of evil, disobedient to parents, foolish, faithless, heartless, ruthless" (RSV). The picture is spectacularly and painfully clear.

2. Sin Is a Deceitful Monster

Paul personifies sin as a deceptive monster that wrecks and destroys. Internally, the beast destroys the unity and wholeness and integrity of persons. Externally, it destroys the relationship between persons. Most important of all, it destroys relationship with God.

Paul summarizes this power of sin as the power of death. The vivid language of Rom. 7:10-11 captures the essence of it: "The very commandment which promised life proved to be death to me. For sin, finding opportunity in the commandment, deceived me and by it killed me" (RSV).

In the eighth chapter of Romans, Paul describes the core problem as a defiant rebellion against God. The self, controlled by the monster of sin, is not only unwilling to submit to the rule of God and enjoy a relationship with Him but also *incapable* of submitting to the will of God. This perverse incapacity to submit to God's law sabotages the potential of any relationship with Him—and thus sabotages the potential for any genuine spiritual development or holy living.

3. Sin Works from the Inside Out

The representation of sin as a death-dealing ogre does not mean the situation is hopeless. Sin is not some external force. "Sin does not exist independently of man. It is furthermore not to be regarded as some flawed or defective part of human nature . . . So we must not so much speak about sin as about man as sinner."[7] The essence of sin is an attitude of rebellion that defies God and replaces submissiveness with a trust in self.

> **When we lose the ability
> to trust God and others,
> we die in isolation.**

Mildred Wynkoop writes: "Man's problem is not a substructure of some alien substance clinging to his soul but his own alienation from God."[8] She defines sin as "simply the absence of this relationship [with God] because man has repudiated it. This repudiation is ethical to the core and has consequences in all areas of the rational life of man and reaches into everything man touches. This rupture is a disintegrative force, religiously, in the psyche of the person sinning, in society, in the world, in all the relationships he sustains to person and things."[9]

Like Venetia Flaxton in *Scandalous Risks*, we use elaborate arguments to deny that anything is really wrong. We attempt elaborate deceptions—of others and of ourselves—in order to legitimate our desires. We refuse to admit that the process is destroying us and our relationship with God.

Ultimately the priest forced Venetia to look into the mirror. When she did, she began to recognize and admit the destructive power of the whole situation. It was visible on her face and also in her heart. To what does your face and heart testify?

▶ For Personal Reflection and Action ◀

How Does This Chapter Affect Me?

Sin presents a dark picture—until we consider grace. So read this section in anticipation of the rich gift of God's grace, which occupies our attention in the next chapter.

1. Recognize the Undeniable Nature of Sin

One of the most deceitful aspects of sinfulness is the temptation to disguise the true understanding of sin for our own purposes. Our definitions of sin are affected by many different factors: the definitions (conscious or unconscious) in our families, the connotations of sin in our culture, the specific temptations that have a grip on our own lives.

Explore the effects of such factors on your own definition of sin in your personal journal. As you gain insight and understanding, bring these understandings to the Word of God for correction and clarification.

2. Honestly Assess the Damages in Your Own Life

A person under the power of sin loses the ability to trust. When we lose the ability to trust God and others, we die in isolation. I can still hear the voice of the young man confessing to a small group: "I recall the night I was betrayed by my best friend while still in junior high school. I vowed I would never allow anyone to get near enough to me to betray me in that fashion again. I have kept that promise to this very day. But today, as a result, I am only a semimobile corpse, and for me God is barely warm." Assess the damage of sin in your life.

3. Confess Your Sinful Acts to God

Until we confess our sinfulness, relationship with God is impossible. Apart from the function of grace in our lives, we will never know a developing relationship with God.

The biblical word for repentance includes a sorrow for

sin, a change of mind, and a change of direction. The Bible promises, "If we confess our sins, he is faithful and just, and will forgive our sins and cleanse us from all unrighteousness" (1 John 1:9, RSV).

4. Bible Study
Prayerfully consider these passages:
Gal. 3:22; 5:16-17; 6:7-8
Rom. 3:9-26
Eph. 1:7-8; 2:3-10

5. Make This Prayer Your Own
Lord Jesus, here I am, a lost creature, an enemy to God, under His wrath and curse. Wilt Thou, Lord, undertake for me, reconcile me to God, and save my soul? Do not, Lord, refuse me, for if Thou refuse me, to whom then shall I go? . . .

Since I come at the command of the Father, reject me not. Lord, help me. Lord, save me.

I come, Lord, I believe, Lord. I throw myself upon Thy grace and mercy. I cast myself upon Thy blood. Do not refuse me. Here I will stay. On Thee I will trust, and rest, and venture myself. On Thee I lay my hope for pardon, for life, for salvation. If I perish, I perish on Thy shoulders. If I sink, I sink in Thy vessel. If I die, I die at Thy door . . .

O most holy God, I beseech Thee, accept the poor prodigal prostrating himself at Thy door.

—John Wesley

6. In the Coming Days, Make This Hymn Your Constant Companion
"I Lay My Sins on Jesus" (Hymn 340 in *Sing to the Lord*)

Saving grace makes spiritual formation possible.
Sanctifying grace makes the potential for growth
in Christlikeness as broad as the horizon
and as deep as the sea.

3

O to Grace
How Great a Debtor!

I was raised on a farm in North Dakota. Although a river bisected our farm, I never learned to swim. My mother's fear of water seeped into my psyche, and I studiously avoided learning how to swim. Well, I did learn to "swim"—close enough to the shore to be able to drop one foot to the bottom at a moment's notice. Technically, I doubt that could really be called swimming.

For a long while I tried to organize my spiritual life in the same way I "swam." I trusted God, but I always prepared to rescue myself—just in case. Technically, I doubt that could really be called living by grace alone.

THE CRUCIAL ROLE OF GRACE

From beginning to end, spiritual formation is the work of grace and grace alone. To lose sight of that basic truth undermines and perverts all spiritual formation. The Wesleyan way of spiritual formation underlines the critical role of grace. It is a radical optimism that grows directly out of the biblical understanding of grace.

The cardinal role of grace is clearly visible in the second chapter of Ephesians. The apostle acknowledges the devastating consequences of sin—with the resultant devastation and paralysis. The entrance of grace, however, makes a decisive difference:

> But God, who is rich in mercy, out of the great love with which he loved us, even when we were dead through our trespasses, made us alive together with Christ (by GRACE you have been saved), and raised us up with him, and made us sit with him in the heavenly places in Christ Jesus, that in the coming ages he might show the immeasurable riches of his GRACE in kindness toward us in Christ Jesus. For by GRACE you have been saved through faith; and this is not your own doing, it is the gift of God—not because of works, lest any man should boast *(Eph. 2:4-9, RSV, emphasis added)*.

The death-dealing power of sin disrupts all possibilities of spiritual formation, but the powerful dynamic of God's grace reverses that destruction and brings radical optimism.

1. Grace Functions Before We Accept Christ

Grace functions in our lives from the very beginning. Even during our times of rebellion God is at work. The possibility of repentance and return to God is itself a gift of grace. Paul voiced that idea in Romans in these words: "While we were still weak, at the right time Christ died for the ungodly. . . . But God proves his love for us in that while we still were sinners Christ died for us" (5:6, 8).

John Wesley helped us understand the crucial role of God's prevenient grace. The "freedom for God" was destroyed in the Fall, he said. Original sin, sometimes known as total depravity, destroyed any possibility of spiritual development or a relationship with God, apart from grace.

The restoration of "freedom for God" by grace enables us to respond to God's offer of salvation in Christ. Prevenient grace is best understood in our own lives in retrospect. When we look back over our lives we can see the diverse ways in which God was preparing us all along.

Students in a class on spiritual formation were invited to list their five most significant encounters with Christ. One student was amazed to discover that three of those five encounters had occurred prior to his conversion. What a gracious God we serve!

> **The crucial encounter with Christ in saving grace is the exclusive entrance into spiritual formation.**

What an encouragement to know
> that our first small baby steps toward God are enabled by His grace!
> that God's preparatory grace is extended to everyone!
> that when we share our faith in Christ with another person, God has already been at work in that person's life!
> that whenever the gospel is presented in any medium, the listeners have already been the recipients of grace!

An anonymous poet wrote:
> *I sought the Lord, and afterward I knew*
> *He moved my soul to seek Him, seeking me.*
> *It was not I that found, O Saviour true;*
> *No, I was found of thee.*

2. Grace Functions When Sins Are Forgiven

Recognition of the damage of sin in our lives brings us to the only possible solution in the presence of a holy God. We can only acknowledge our helplessness and confess our sins to Him.

Paul communicates the good news of forgiveness of sins with the metaphor of reconciliation in Rom. 5:10-11: "For if while we were enemies we were reconciled to God by the death of his Son, much more, now that we are reconciled, shall we be saved by his life. Not only so, but we also rejoice in God through our Lord Jesus Christ, through whom we have now received our reconciliation" (RSV).

Reconciliation has profound results on a number of different levels: (1) between God and human beings (Rom. 5:1; Gal. 5:22; Col. 3:15); (2) between persons (Eph. 2:12-17; 4:3-6); and (3) on the cosmic level (Col. 1:20).

Paul uses a wide range of the metaphors to describe the wonder of God's work for us in Christ. Meditate on the power of the language in Col. 2:13-15 (NIV): "When you were dead in your sins and in the uncircumcision of your sinful nature, God made you alive with Christ. He forgave us all our sins, having canceled the written code, with its regulations, that was against us and that stood opposed to us; he took it away, nailing it to the cross. And having disarmed the powers and authorities, he made a public spectacle of them, triumphing over them by the cross."

First, he uses the metaphor of restoration of life—"God made you alive with Christ." The Gospel of John uses the language of rebirth to capture the same theme. Small wonder that we used the words *born again* and *born from above* to try to express the grace-filled gift of forgiveness of sins. Creedal formulas use the technical word *regeneration* to try to capture it.

Second, Paul uses the metaphor of forgiveness of sin— "he forgave us all our sins." Notice that God is the subject of the sentence—it could only be grace! To try to convey the meaning of forgiveness, Paul adds some additional metaphors. He states the certificate of indebtedness that stood against us in the records has been wiped clean— erased, cancelled. He then speaks of the disarming of all the powers and authorities that keep us imprisoned in sin. The powerless powers are put on public display as being harmless. Christ has triumphed over them in the Cross.

What a celebration of the freedom grace provides! Paul celebrates it in Gal. 5:1: "It is for freedom that Christ has set us free. Stand firm, then, and do not let yourselves be burdened again by a yoke of slavery" (NIV).

Accepting Christ as Savior (another way of expressing these ideas that underline the critical function of faith) is such a profound moment that life is forever different. The removal of the guilt and the penalty for the sins that are inked on our side of the ledger opens up possibilities of spiritual formation. The crucial and dramatic encounter with saving grace in Christ is the exclusive entrance to spiritual growth!

> **While some traditions talk about the "whitewash job" the Atonement accomplishes, Wesley takes the biblical promises of sanctification literally.**

Restoration to relationship is only the beginning of the work of grace in our lives. The new viewpoint creates the possibility for grace to function in every area of our lives. An exuberant young Christian was testifying to the tremendous change in his life and said: "When I accepted Christ as Savior, it affected every faucet of my personality." He meant to say "facet" instead of "faucet," but I like the idea. Every faucet of our being spews new water after Jesus comes into our lives!

3. Grace Functions When We Are Sanctified

The optimism of grace in the Wesleyan mode does not end with reconciliation through the forgiveness of sins. While some theological traditions talk about the "whitewash job" the Atonement accomplishes (one writer even uses the analogy of snow covering the junkyard to make it look beautiful), Wesley takes the biblical promises of sanctification literally.

> The New Testament and John Wesley speak with one voice in proclaiming that the great purpose of redemption is to restore man to the image of God . . . The total process of sanctification from its beginning in the new birth, its

"perfection in love" at entire sanctification, and its progressive development toward final salvation has as its objective the restoring of man to his original destiny.[1]

The grace that prepares us to hear and respond to God's call and the saving grace that brings rebirth and reconciliation lead directly into the sanctifying grace in which the image of God is restored more fully.

Belonging to God Exclusively

Sanctifying grace enables us to regain the possibility of belonging exclusively to God and to Him alone. When we have submitted to His perfect will and have dedicated ourselves to do His will without any loopholes or escape clauses in the contract, then we are free to love God with our whole heart and soul and mind and strength (Mark 12:30). The perverted self-love that led to evasion, denial, and deceit is dissolved through the atoning work of Christ. Obedience to the perfect will of God is now the primary goal. The problem of inner rebellion has been solved at the Cross.

Freedom from Sinful Self-domination

Sanctifying grace also frees us from the devastating condition of self-domination. The freedom from the domination of sin is a fundamental freedom: "For if we have been united with him in a death like his, we shall certainly be united with him in a resurrection like his. We know that our old self was crucified with him so that the sinful body might be destroyed, and we might no longer be enslaved to sin. For he who has died is freed from sin" (Rom. 6:5-7, RSV).

The language of the New Testament announces a powerful and complete victory over sin and its domination. The texts include decisive verbs such as "destroy," "purge," "cleanse," and "abolish." "There is therefore now no condemnation for those who are in Christ Jesus. For the law of the Spirit of life in Christ Jesus has set you free from the law of sin and death" (Rom. 8:1-2, RSV).

Robin Maas, in *Crucified Love: The Practice of Christian Perfection*, summarizes this wonderful work of grace in these terms: "The consequences of original sin infect every layer of our being . . . The sin that festers at the center of our being can only be eradicated in the furnace of God's love."[2]

The Grace of Christian Perfection

The language of "going on to perfection"—which John Wesley preferred—is thoroughly scriptural. Jesus shocked His hearers with similar language. When Jesus spoke to the rich young ruler, He said: "If you want to be perfect, go, sell your possessions and give to the poor, and you will have treasure in heaven. Then come, follow me" (Matt. 19:21, NIV). The young man went away with a sad face.

Robin Maas captures well the New Testament concept of Christian perfection: "Whereas the modern personality seeks fulfillment through an *uncovering* or process of self-discovery, the early Christians sought fulfillment—or rather, completion—through a process of formation, that is, through a kind of shaping or molding of the self . . . The model governing the shaping was Jesus Christ."[3]

> **The radical optimism of grace of Wesleyan spirituality is possible because of the energizing presence of the Holy Spirit.**

The writer of Hebrews spends a great deal of time talking about the perfection of Jesus himself. The Great Day of Atonement, according to Leviticus, required the most elaborate preparations for qualifying the high priest to appear in the holy of holies. The writer to the Hebrews announces the perfect qualification of Jesus to be the High Priest in order to solve the festering problem of our sinful nature (Heb. 5:7-9).

Jesus, the perfectly qualified High Priest of our salvation, provides sanctifying grace that we may be perfectly qualified to "approach the throne of grace with boldness so that we may receive mercy and find grace to help in time of need" (Heb. 4:16, RSV).

John Wesley taught that perfection was the humble, gentle, patient love of God, and our neighbor, "ruling our tempers, words, and actions." Robin Maas summarizes the understanding of *perfection* in Wesley.

By "perfection" Wesley meant that same single-minded devotion to God that he first found in Taylor and Law—an absolute purity of *intention* that expressed itself in love for the good and an abhorrence of sin. A perfect Christian by this definition was not someone freed from the limitations of the human condition; . . . Rather, perfection, as John Wesley understood it, was reflected in a purity of intention toward God and conferred the freedom to stop committing known or *conscious* sins. This purity of intention is itself not the consequence for human effort, it is the gift of God's overflowing, prevenient grace. Perfection is the work of the Spirit *in* us—a work that requires our full cooperation if the hoped-for transformation is to occur.[4]

Appropriate Relationships to Neighbor and World

Sanctifying grace enables us to follow the second great commandment as well. According to Jesus, our first obligation is to love God and the second is to "love your neighbor as yourself" (Mark 12:31).

The divisive power of sin that drove wedges between God and us also created divisions in relationships on the human plane. Now sanctifying grace again makes us free to love each other. The whole possibility of the unity of the Body of Christ is wrapped up in this wonderful provision of sanctifying grace.

Life-style of Integrity and Ethical Consistency

Sanctifying grace makes possible a new depth of obedience to God marked by integrity and ethical consistency. The New Testament marks out that pattern of life from beginning to end. Jesus, in the Sermon on the Mount, sets a high standard when He says: "Be perfect, therefore, as your heavenly Father is perfect" (Matt. 5:48). He is echoing the great commandment from the Levitical code: "For I am the Lord your God; sanctify yourselves therefore, and be holy, for I am holy" (Lev. 11:44).

Paul, in each of his Epistles, holds up a high standard of living for the person who loves God exclusively. For example, after a long list of the characteristics of life apart from the Spirit in the fifth chapter of Galatians, Paul lists the distinguishing marks of the Christian: "But the fruit of the Spirit is love, joy, peace, patience, kindness, goodness, faithfulness, gentleness, self-control . . . And those who belong to Christ Jesus have crucified the flesh with its passions and desires. If we live by the Spirit, let us also walk by the Spirit" (Gal. 5:22-25, RSV).

Profound gratitude for these new freedoms under grace characterizes every level of sanctified living. Small wonder that the new life in the Spirit is marked by inner and outer harmony!

Grace at Work Through the Holy Spirit

The radical optimism of Wesleyan spirituality is possible because of the energizing and dynamic presence of the Holy Spirit in the life of the person who is sanctified. "For Wesley, the goal of the Spirit was nothing less than a total transformation of both the individual and the society. Fallen humanity was called to holiness of heart and holiness of life—to inward perfection and a visible, external expression of love for neighbor that Wesley liked to call 'social holiness.'"[5]

All these characteristics of the new life in the Spirit are made possible by grace. Apart from the grace imparted to us by God through His Holy Spirit, we are bankrupt and broken. Living by grace, we are freed to live a life pleasing to God, open to minister and serve those around us, ready to live in harmony with ourselves and our world. We have then found the path—the path that leads to the highway of holiness.

FINDING SAVING AND SANCTIFYING GRACE

1. How Do I Find Saving Grace?

God is eager to save you from your sins and bring you into a redemptive relationship with Him, that is, to give you eternal life. There is nothing we can do to earn or deserve salvation. "For by grace are ye saved through faith; and that not of yourselves: it is the gift of God: Not of works, lest any man should boast" (Eph. 2:8-9, KJV). Nevertheless, we must open our hearts to receive the gift of grace.

For 2,000 years, sinners have experienced saving grace by opening their hearts to God in this scriptural way:

A. Confess That You Are a Guilty Sinner

"All we like sheep have gone astray; we have turned every one to his own way" (Isa. 53:6, KJV). "For all have sinned, and come short of the glory of God" (Rom. 3:23, KJV).

B. To Your Confession Add Repentance

That is, "forsake" your sins. Repentance means to turn around and go the other direction. Renounce your sinful ways and turn to God. "Except ye repent ye shall all likewise perish" (Luke 13:3, KJV). "The Lord is . . . not willing that any should perish, but that all should come to repentance" (2 Pet. 3:9, KJV). "God . . . commandeth all men every where to repent" (Acts 17:30, KJV).

C. Believe in Jesus Christ as Your Savior

Believe that Jesus Christ died for you and that God's love and grace is extended even to a sinner like you. "For God so loved the world, that he gave his only begotten Son, that whosoever believeth in him should not perish, but have everlasting life" (John 3:16, KJV).

Accept Him as Savior and as Lord. Receive His gift of saving grace, and put your trust in Him. From this day forward, do not trust in your skills, your bank account, or your career. Instead your hope and your trust will be in Jesus Christ.

D. Receive the Witness of the Spirit

The Spirit of God gives us a deep inner assurance that our sins are forgiven and that we have been adopted into the family of God. "The Spirit itself beareth witness with our spirit, that we are the children of God" (Rom. 8:16, KJV).

2. How Do I Find Sanctifying Grace?

A. Know That It Is God's Will

"This is the will of God, even your sanctification" (1 Thess. 4:3, KJV). Align your hope and expectation with Paul's prayer for the Thessalonian believers: "May God himself, the God of peace, sanctify you through and through" (1 Thess. 5:23, NIV).

B. Invite God to Prepare Your Heart

God will faithfully lead you to see the depths of inbred sin—that inward sinfulness that wars against the soul even after acts of sin have been forgiven. He will use the deep hunger of your own soul to lead you. When He has brought you to the place where you love Him with all of your heart, mind, soul, and strength, He bestows sanctifying grace, purifying your heart and filling you with His love. The promise is sure—"If we walk in the light as He is in the light, . . . the blood of Jesus Christ His Son cleanses us from all sin" (1 John 1:7, NKJV).

C. Make Your Consecration Complete

Complete consecration to God is not easy, but it is the only access into the freedom and security that grace offers. For me, entering the narrow gate of entire consecration was complicated by years of role-playing in the church. Acting piously at times, playing rebel at others was such a charade that I began fooling myself. Finally one day at the altar of Nazarene Theological Seminary, I was able to genuinely dedicate myself to God. I stepped within the boundaries of His love—boundaries forever etched in red at the Cross. I have experienced the radical optimism the Bible describes and Wesley preached!

D. Expect Sanctifying Grace Instantaneously by Faith

It sounds like a gradual process of growth at first, and it does require time for God to prepare the believer's heart. But the testimony of God's people throughout the centuries almost always declares that sanctifying grace comes instantaneously, after the believer has once and for all made consecration complete and opened the very depths of his heart to the purging fire of the Spirit.

E. Patiently Follow the Hunger of Your Soul

If you follow the deepest hunger of your soul, God will lead you into sanctifying grace and a rich fellowship with Him. Seek with your whole heart, without fretting or tormenting yourself. Resist efforts of zealous persons to get you to claim the blessing prematurely.

Meanwhile, do not put your Christian life on hold. John Wesley taught that the way to "wait" for entire sanctification was to throw yourself into "acts of piety" (prayer, worship, hearing sermons, Communion) and "acts of mercy" (feeding the hungry, instructing the weak, clothing the naked, visiting the sick).

You can trust God to give you His sanctifying grace—the grace Christ provided through the Cross.

▶ For Personal Reflection and Action ◀

1. Bible Study
Read these scriptures with an open heart:
Eph. 2:1-10
Gal. 5:1, 22-25
2 Thess. 5:23-24

2. The Sinner's Prayer

If you are unsaved, confess all known sin to God. Confess your spiritual condition and your need to be rescued by Jesus Christ.

Two things you must know: (1) You are a sinner, and (2) Jesus Christ is the Savior.

Use the "Jesus prayer" as the "starter" for your prayer of confession. "Lord Jesus Christ, Son of God, Savior, have mercy on me, a sinner."

If you are already a born-again Christian, offer a prayer of thanksgiving for God's saving grace.

3. A Prayer for Sanctifying Grace

If you are already saved, and if you feel led by the Spirit to do so, make this prayer for sanctifying grace your own and dare to believe that God will hear and answer:

O God, I open my heart to its depths before you. Cleanse by the fire of Your Spirit anything that is unlike Christ. Purge my attitudes, my spirit, my affections. Consume all my sinfulness.

Fill me with Your love until I love even those who persecute or mistreat me. Make me a flame of divine love.

Take all that is mine—I hold nothing back. I claim no right to my wealth, position, or reputation. I give you my body, my soul, my freedom, my friends, and my life. Do with me as You wish. I wish only to know You better and to serve You throughout eternity. In the name of Jesus my Savior, I pray, Amen.

If you have already received sanctifying grace, make the preceding prayer an act of rededication.

Make this hymn part of your devotions this week: "Whiter than Snow" (Hymn 513 in *Sing to the Lord*).

PART **II**

Finding Resources for the Journey

... growing in Christlikeness,
using the spiritual disciplines ...

Watch therefore. For life in time is not a stumbling
from one ecstatic epiphany to another. The
enormous task is to keep your eyes open,
your wick trimmed, your lamp filled.
—Virginia Stem Owens
And the Trees Clap Their Hands

Prayer, . . . searching the Scriptures, . . . and receiving
the Lord's supper . . . these we believe to be ordained
of God, as the ordinary channels of conveying
his grace to the souls of men.
—John Wesley
"The Means of Grace"

The aim and substance of spiritual life is not fasting,
prayer, hymn singing, frugal living, and so forth.
Rather, it is the effective and full enjoyment
of active love of God and humankind.
—Dallas Willard
The Spirit of the Disciplines

Introduction to Part II

SPIRITUAL DISCIPLINES: THE MEANS OF GRACE

The apostle Paul testified: "But by the grace of God I am what I am, and his grace toward me was not in vain. On the contrary, I worked harder than any of them, though it was not I, but the grace of God which is with me" (1 Cor. 15:10, RSV). He was quick to recognize that the gifts of God's grace were the originating source and sustaining force of his whole life. He was quick to acknowledge that his whole life was a product of grace and grace alone.

If spiritual formation at its core is a product of grace, where do we turn to find resources for the journey? How do the disciplines and grace intersect? If the relationship is a pure gift of grace, why are disciplines necessary?

When we study Jesus as our model and the acknowledged master of the spiritual life, we immediately see that, as Dallas Willard says: "The activities constituting the disciplines *have no value in themselves*. The aim and substance of spiritual life is not fasting, prayer, hymn singing, frugal living, and so forth. Rather, it is the effective and full enjoyment of active love of God and humankind in all the daily rounds of normal existence where we are placed." He goes on to declare that the spiritually advanced person is not the one who engages in lots and lots of disciplines, that people who think they are spiritually superior because they make a practice of a discipline such as fasting or silence or frugality are entirely missing the point.[1]

At one stage I began to think that indulgence in spiritual disciplines was even a disguised form of selfishness.

In a period of silence in group worship the Spirit clearly led me to recognize the issues involved. Later that day I wrote the following words in my journal: "To nurture one's self is through grace and discipline to create optimum conditions in which the voice of God, the call of Christ to the Kingdom, the enabling work of the Holy Spirit, and the needs of one's world can be brought into effective juxtaposition, creative tension, and reinforcing rhythms which are context-specific and personality-specific."

The disciplines are not ends in themselves but create the conditions in which grace may flow more freely. The disciplines are, in fact, only "means of grace."

John Wesley regularly spoke about the "means of grace" through which God forms and guides our lives for the sake of the Kingdom: "By 'means of grace' I understand outward signs, words, or actions ordained of God, and appointed for this end, to be the ordinary channels whereby he might convey to men, preventing, justifying, or sanctifying grace."[2] He understood that there was no magical or mechanical disbursement of grace in such practices, but that God uses them to nurture and sustain our relationship with Him and to form us spiritually.

Our purpose in Part II is to identify the foundational disciplines that God uses to dispense grace into our lives. Different personalities will receive grace through these disciplines in differing ways as the Holy Spirit uniquely suits them to our lives and circumstances. It is *crucial* that these foundational disciplines become a central part of the strategies of spiritual formation.

Recognizing that all spiritual formation grows out of a relationship with God, *the* foundational discipline through which grace flows into our lives is worship. The related means of grace are study of the Word of God, prayer, meditation, and journaling. Pay special attention to chapter 8, which focuses upon the distractions that ought to be removed in order to allow grace to fashion our lives.

By definition, relationships vary from person to person dependent upon background and personality. The wonder of God's grace is that each of us is permitted to grow in relationship with God in light of our preferences and backgrounds and distinctiveness—whether in worship or prayer or journaling or Bible reading.

**Worship is the essential and crucial means of grace
that colors and focuses all other means of grace.**

4

Meeting God in Worship

Fifty percent of church members in the United States do
not attend worship services with any regularity. Any boast
they may make about dedication to God is contradicted by
their practice.

Worship is crucial to any pattern of spiritual formation. It is a revolutionary and subversive activity in our
contemporary world. Annie Dillard wrote: "Ushers should
issue life preservers and signal flares; they should lash us
to our pews. For . . . the waking God may draw us out to
where we can never return."[1]

A couple of years ago I was reflecting upon the patterns of my life in the previous decade. I was aware of a
deep and abiding healing at work in my life. I thought I
understood many parts of that process. Suddenly it
dawned upon me that healing had been particularly mediated through participation in the Lord's Supper. I could
identify at least a dozen different Communion services in
which the Lord's presence had deeply touched and redi-
rected my life. Praise be to God!

The primacy of worship in the life of the church has
often been noted in literature across the centuries. It has

proven far more difficult to carry that primacy out in practice. A wise man once said: "The missing jewel of evangelicalism is worship."[2]

SOME DEFINITIONS OF WORSHIP

In order to understand the role of worship in spiritual formation, let us review some definitions of worship. Here is William Temple's definition:

> To worship God is:
> To quicken the conscience by the holiness of God,
> To feed the mind with the truth of God,
> To purge the imagination by the beauty of God,
> To open the heart to the love of God,
> To devote the will to the purpose of God.[3]

Evelyn Underhill wrote: "Worship, in all its grades and kinds, is the response of the creature to the Eternal."[4] Again, the emphasis is upon the orientation of our worship. One of the German words frequently encountered in discussions about worship is *Gottesdienst*.[5] The word connotes the service we owe to God. The English word *liturgy* originally meant the service a citizen owed the society of which he was a part. When the word is used with reference to worship, it refers to the work the people owe—to God.

Robert Webber's revision of *Worship Is a Verb* provides a fascinating approach to worship through eight principles.

1. Worship celebrates Christ—God's definitive work in Christ.

2. Worship tells and acts out the Christ-event.

3. In the process of worship God speaks again to touch and heal and make whole.

4. Worship is an act of communication, interaction with God. The divine presence confirms God's people in faith and community.

5. In worship we respond to God and to each other.

6. Return the worship to the people. A passive approach to worship is a denial of the divine action in our midst. Participatory worship is demanded.

7. All creation joins in worship.

8. Worship as a way of life. Worship is not simply something we do on Sunday, but must eventuate in a way of life—until our whole lives are expressions of gratitude and celebration to God.[6]

John Burkhart calls worship "the celebrative response to what God has done, is doing, and promises to do."[7]

THE BIBLICAL PERSPECTIVE ON WORSHIP

There is a wide variety of words for worship in the Bible. The words include ideas such as bow down, serve, worship, make a sacrifice, reverence, and fear. The Old Testament is filled with invitations to worship. The holy God calls for a holy people who worship Him in fear and trembling. The Psalmist is particularly vocal about his struggles and his complaints, but he also repeatedly moves into worship.

> **The failure to prepare heart and mind and body for worship is to render oneself tone deaf to the things of the Spirit.**

The 96th psalm is one of my favorites. Verse 1, 9, and 10 (NIV) read: "Sing to the Lord a new song; sing to the Lord, all the earth. . . . Worship the Lord in the splendor of his holiness; tremble before him, all the earth. Say among the nations, 'The Lord reigns.'"

The message of the New Testament is that access to the divine presence has now been wonderfully enriched and enabled by the death and resurrection of Christ. Jesus himself identifies the central text of the Old Testament as: "Love the Lord your God with all your heart, and with all your soul, and with all your mind" (Mark 12:30). Then He immediately cites love of neighbor as the second great commandment.

The first day of the week has forever turned into a worship celebration by the resurrection of Christ. It became known as The Lord's Day. Love feasts and the Lord's Supper become the "basis and goal of every gathering."[8]

The worshiping community in the Book of Acts is at the heart and core of the outreach of the Early Church. The early Christians were willing to take great risks to be together in worship.

The writer to the Hebrews particularly underlines the access to God as "the new and living way" (10:20). Now we may "draw near to God with a sincere heart in full assurance of faith" (v. 22, NIV). Worship has now become a celebration of the completed work of Christ for us. The trembling fear breaks into confidence and freedom to come before the throne of God boldly (4:16).

When the final catastrophes of Revelation begin to move toward a crescendo, so does worship. The climax of the end of the age will be a mighty worship service celebrating the final victory over evil at the Marriage Supper of the Lamb.

WORSHIP AS A MEANS OF GRACE

One of the exquisite joys of life is participation in a worship service in which the presence of God is as *visible* as the persons with whom we worship. Heart and mind and soul and body are all affected. We depart with the assurance that life will be different as a result of this encounter with God. We have truly experienced worship as a "means of grace."

When we approach worship as a duty or as a performance, the possibility of sensitivity to grace is greatly reduced. To come to worship in anticipation of receiving grace for immediate needs changes perspective and process.

Wesley included the Lord's Supper in his list of the instituted means of grace. He understands *instituted* to mean that they are means of grace that have been specifically grounded in the instructions of Christ. Over the centuries the Church has designated a wide variety of means of grace in recognition of the many and various ways in which God works. God often touches our lives in unexpected ways through unexpected means.

Rob Staples offers a helpful perspective on the means of grace: "All means of grace must be defined by the Christ event. The Word (both written and preached) is a means of grace because its center is in Christ, the Living Word. Prayer is a means of grace because it is prayer in Christ's name. Certainly the sacraments are inseparable from the work of Christ . . . Christ is thus the ruling power of the means of grace."[9]

Worship that does not result in praise is not worthy of the name.

If Christ is "the ruling power of the means of grace," then worship lies at the center of all means of grace. All aspects of the life of the church (evangelism, education, compassionate ministry, etc.) find their center and definition in worship.

To neglect worship as the fundamental procedure in spiritual formation is to invite spiritual anemia. Spiritual formation calls for time before God in community. As we pray together, we grow together. In the days when our lives are dry and barren, community prayer enriches and carries us. On those days when our spiritual life is vibrant, we enrich and carry others.

The Body of Christ was designed by God himself for worship. Paul spoke of the community in terms of the Temple: "Don't you know that you yourselves are God's temple and that God's Spirit lives in you? . . . God's temple is sacred, and you are that temple" (1 Cor. 3:16-17, NIV).

Worship for spiritual growth is the place where love makes us one in the presence of God. Maria Harris wrote:

"The ministry of community . . . is the ministry that moves us toward the healing of division, toward overcoming brokenness, and ultimately toward achieving wholeness."[10]

Receiving Grace Through Worship

Most writings on the means of grace point out that the process of receiving grace is not automatic. Rob Staples reminds us: "Wesley was careful to make clear that the means of grace . . . have value to us only when we see that our salvation . . . is the work of God alone. That is the meaning of grace—God does for us what we cannot do for ourselves."[11]

1. Preparation for Worship

Following custom, I walked reverently to my pew. I sat down, bowed my head, and began preparing my heart for worship. A fellow parishioner gave me a shove with her hand and said, "Wake up, the service hasn't started yet." I was frustrated at the interruption and saddened for the person who came into worship with so little preparation.

To understand the worship service as a meeting with the Creator God of the universe should create a certain amount of awe. To understand worship as an opportunity to receive grace for my deepest need should create a sense of anticipation.

For the last 15 years I have been participating in an early Sunday morning prayer time. A group of us meets at 7 A.M. to share our common burdens, to strengthen each other's faith, and especially to pray for the services of the day. We always pray for the pastor—often laying hands on him in anticipation of the day.

I find that these early Sunday morning prayer times have become a special preparation for worship. They help me enter the sanctuary with a quiet heart and mind. I pray that I may be able to offer appropriate worship to God. I pray that I may be open to the voice and grace of God, to the opportunity to be a vehicle of God's grace to those who worship with me.

I am convinced that failure to prepare heart and mind and body for worship is the leading reason why so many evangelical services are routine and boring. Unprepared persons are usually tone deaf to the things of the Spirit.

2. Praise and Singing

One of the geniuses of worship in the Wesleyan format is the significant role of music. John Wesley's ability to theologize and understand the impact of the Word of God upon life was matched by the ability of his brother, Charles, to put those great ideas into song. Like Martin Luther during the Reformation, the Wesleys literally used theology in song to save England from the revolution that ravaged Europe.

The writer to the Hebrews wrote: "Through Jesus, therefore, let us continually offer to God a sacrifice of praise—the fruit of lips that confess his name" (13:15, NIV).

Worship begins in praise to the God who has lavished His grace upon us in Christ Jesus. Worship that does not result in praise is not worthy of the name.

God has graciously provided a wide variety of music as vehicles of praise. In the Nazarene Theological Seminary chapel, the sound of the student body singing "And Can It Be?" is enough to thrill the heart of the deadest soul. The memory of a college choir singing the third verse of "It Is Well with My Soul" still brings joy to my heart. Authentic praise flows from the heart of the persons who have walked through the valley of the shadow of death and found the Savior there.

I have been deeply moved by the nature of praise in Walter Brueggemann's study of the Psalms. He discusses the way in which life tends to rob us of hope and praise. He talks about praise as "world making" in the midst of the current tension. "Praise has the power to transform the pain. But, conversely, the present pain also keeps the act of praise honest."[12] The pain creates the context in which we dare to trust God to do a "new thing" for us. Brueggeman declares: "Thus I propose that *access into life is mostly through the resistant door of pain* . . . Praise always happens midst the irreducible reality of pain. The *pain at the center of praise* has theological warrant in Israel in the cries of hurt, rage, doubt, vengeance, and isolation. Most importantly, they are cries, not buried, not stifled, but cries passionately addressed out of the reality of life."[13]

> **What a moment in the church and in creation, when the church sings its way into an improvised fresh future!**

If Israel can sing to the Lord in the beauty of holiness (Psalm 96), the new creature in Christ can sing and praise and celebrate with even greater depth. The Cross and the open tomb are demonstrations that God is not yet through working in our midst.

"What a moment in the church and in creation, when the church sings its way into an improvised fresh future! . . . It is a moment of threat and of healing, of breaking down and building up, of weeping and laughing, of mourning and dance, of throwing away and keeping, of seeking and losing. It is a joyful noise—for all things new."[14]

3. Praying Together

Authentic worship includes some marvelous moments of prayer. When the minister prays the invocation and invites the whole world to be silent as we take our places in preparation to worship God, we are joining the millions who have worshiped since time began. It is a phenomenal moment!

When the congregation joins together in the prayer our Lord taught us to pray, there is a blending of minds and hearts that is not found outside the worship experience. One of my sacred memories of worship came on a day when we had studied the Lord's Prayer together. We came to the realization that every verb in the prayer was in the imperative (command). So we shouted the Lord's Prayer together at the top of our lungs. What a worship experience!

How powerful it is to be included in the prayer of confession the pastor prays for us! We know in our heart of hearts that we have not been able to live up to the ideals we have for ourselves. To own that gap and to understand that grace touches our lives at that point as well is an exquisite moment of worship.

The pastoral prayer has long been a joy for me. As the pastor serves as priest and carries the whole congregation into the very presence of God, we share our joys and our sorrows and pains. The power of His grace touches us all anew!

4. The Preaching of the Word

The contemporary evangelical church appears to be losing the skill of really listening to the Word of God. We have lost our reverence for it. Thus it ceases to be a means of grace for us.

Worship in the Protestant context is unthinkable without the centrality of the Scripture. The grace of God is mediated to us through the preaching of His Word. We must recover the art of listening to the ministry of the Word as a means of receiving grace.

The critics of preaching, those "carping censures of the world," to use Shakespeare's phrase, seem to be blithely unaware of the high place preaching has in Christian tradition. Dietrich Bonhoeffer declared: "The proclaimed Word is the Incarnate Christ himself . . . the preached Christ is the historical Christ and the present Christ . . . walking through His congregation as the Word."[15]

"So identified is Jesus the Word with the word of preaching," writes Richard Lischer, "that the one proclaimed once again becomes the proclaimer. Insofar as preaching . . . offers the life of God in Christ, it is Jesus himself who is the preacher."[16]

The Bible is our record of divine history. It is our witness to Jesus Christ. It is our guidebook and our hope. It should determine the content of our worship and direct the affairs of daily living.

We must echo Wesley's cry: "O Give me that Book!" There is special grace available in the hearing of the Word in the context of worship!

5. The Sacraments

Robert Webber writes: "I often counsel students and friends who are facing difficult times in their lives to *flee to the Eucharist*. Bread and wine are God's signs. They are what John Calvin called *pledges, testimonies*, and *signs* of God's grace and love toward us."[17] A little later he writes: "We need to come to the Table of the Lord with a sense of anticipation, believing that the Lord will meet us there in a unique way, that he will heal our hurts, bind up our wounds, and minister to our needs."[18]

Rob Staples calls the sacraments "visible words" and "operative symbols." By "operative symbols" he means "to affirm not only that they *proclaim* a truth but that through them God *performs* an act of grace corresponding to that truth."[19]

Overreacting to the theology of the Eucharist from the Roman Catholic church, we have robbed the Lord's Table of its significance. We say, in effect: "This is only a symbolic process. Nothing really happens here. It is safe to come forward and receive the elements."

In fact, the grace of God is powerfully present at the Lord's Table. As we participate in this rehearsal of God's definitive acts in Christ, we open ourselves for God to flood our lives anew with His grace. "And *with* faith, the sacraments accomplish what they were designed to do— impart to the believer the grace of God. The 'outward sign' and the 'inward grace' working together—these are what make a sacrament."[20]

At a retreat, the bread and the juice were offered to us with the words: "Receive this gift of His grace." We responded: "I receive this gift of His grace! May Christ be fully formed in me!" And grace flowed again into our lives.

6. Responding to God and to Each Other

Our overfamiliarity with God has resulted in insensitivity to Him. The failure to recognize God's transcendence has resulted in absence of awe. Our insensitivity to the presence of His Spirit has resulted in dry and mechanical participation in worship.

> **Worship is the rehearsal of what God has done in the past in anticipation of what He is about to do in the immediate future.**

The primary response should be an awareness that we are in the presence of the living God—He who created the universe, He who sent His only Son to die for us, He whose power forever changed the world on that first Easter morning, He who gave us His Holy Spirit on Pentecost so long ago.

As I celebrate the gift of God's presence, I respond to those with whom I worship. I pray and sing and listen as grace flows in and around and through the whole Body of Christ.

Recently I participated in a healing service for one of my colleagues who was facing a dire diagnosis of two kinds of cancer simultaneously. It was a powerful experience for me. I was deeply moved by the divine presence at work.

Six months later we celebrated God's healing in His life when the doctors announced (not without some surprise and attempt to "explain" the previous diagnosis) that he was cancer-free. The praise in the midst of pain was visible again.

7. Corporate and Personal Worship

It remains only to say that corporate worship is the core of spiritual formation. After all, we are the Bride of Christ and the Body of Christ en route to the great Marriage Supper of the Lamb.

Personal patterns of worship are important. Other chapters in this book will explore these important matters. But Maria Harris is correct: "One Christian is no Christian; we go to God together or we do not go at all."[21] This does not mean that private prayer and worship are optional. It merely accents the truth that whatever else the church is, it is a worshiping community.

▶ For Personal Reflection and Action ◀

1. How Imporant Is Corporate Worship?

A. Does God really speak through sermons? Read the quotation from Dietrich Bonhoeffer about preaching. Write it on a card or in your Bible and read it just before the sermon next Sunday. Pray that the Living Word will walk among His people during the preaching part of worship. Write the quote down now so that you will not forget it.

B. Consider what chap. 4 has to say about the sacrament of the Lord's Supper. As you prepare for the next service of Holy Communion, what do you most need to do?

1. Make it a time to confess your sins?

2. Make it a time when you confess your faith in Christ?

3. Make it a time of thanksgiving for Christ's redeeming you through His broken body and shed blood?

4. Make it a time when, as never before, "we are one" at the table of the Lord?

5. All of the above?

    C. In what ways have you experienced the public reading of Scripture, public prayer, and the music of worship to be nurturing experiences?

2. Bible Study

    A. Read carefully Phil. 3:2-16.

    B. In this passage, Paul talks about those "who worship God in spirit, and glory in Christ Jesus" (3:3, RSV). Note the tone, texture, and nature of worship in Paul's testimony. If worship is response to God, in what ways did Paul respond to God as recorded in this passage?

    C. If you were to lead a worship service built around this passage, what hymns or songs would you use? If you were the preacher, what would your sermon title be? If you were to select from Phil. 3:12-16 a call to worship and a benediction, what verses would you use?

3. For Your Journal

    A. In your spiritual life journal make notes about
—something in this study that was new to you
—something you may have rediscovered
—something with which you strongly agree
—something that made you uncomfortable
—something that inspired or comforted you
—something you think the Lord may be calling you to do
    or change

    B. Worth remembering—keep the good stuff. List in your journal a particularly helpful quote from chap. 4 or from the Bible passage studied. Or, why not write the statement most "worth remembering" on a Post-it and stick it on your refrigerator door?

The Spirit of God not only inspired those who wrote it, but continually inspires, supernaturally assists, those that read it with earnest prayer.
—John Wesley
Explanatory Notes upon the New Testament

5

Meeting God in the Word

In a moving passage from *In the Beginning,* Chaim Potok describes the celebration in the synagogue when the annual readings from the Pentateuch (the first five books of the Bible) have been completed. At that celebration, the final words of the Pentateuch and the opening words of Genesis are read in the same service.

In the midst of the liturgy the participants dance with the Torah scrolls. Potok recounts the thoughts of the young Jewish hero as he reflects upon the wonder of holding God's Word, given to Moses at Sinai, in his own arms. He then begins to think about his non-Jewish friends. He starts to wonder how they respond to the Bible. Then he startles himself [and the reader] by asking: "Do Gentiles ever dance with their Bibles?"

We must ask ourselves such questions regularly. What pattern of approach to the Bible will invite grace to shape my life? How does my use of the Bible enrich or detract from the rhythms of the Spirit in my life? How do we allow the Bible to "make us wise"? Are our lives really nurtured by the Word? Since spiritual formation is another way of talking about a relationship with God, the joy of reading His revelation to us should be a high priority.

BIBLE READING AS A STABILIZING FORCE

The Psalmist wrote: "Your word is a lamp to my feet and light to my path" (Ps. 119:105). The whole 119th psalm, in fact, is a celebration of the adequacy and stability the Word provides. Thanks be to God for His Word!

In 2 Timothy, Paul is writing to his young colleague. He warns against the unsettling and destructive influences. Paul reminds Timothy of the stabilizing influence of God's Word in clear language (3:14-17):

> But as for you, continue in what you have learned and firmly believed, knowing from whom you learned it, and how from childhood you have known the sacred writings that are able to instruct you for salvation through faith in Christ Jesus. All scripture is inspired by God and is useful for teaching, for reproof, for correction, and for training in righteousness, so that everyone who belongs to God may be proficient, equipped for every good work.

Do Christians ever dance with their Bibles?

Instruction *for salvation* is a wonderful gift. Knowledge of the way into a relationship with God comes from His revealed Word. What a wonderful privilege it is to have the Scriptures available in so many different translations and paraphrases! There is no excuse for not finding our way to God.

Paul moves from the initial instruction in salvation to some of the further purposes of Scripture. "All scripture . . . is useful for teaching, for reproof, for correction, and for training in righteousness."

The Bible becomes our *teacher* for understanding the nature of a relationship with God. It teaches us the nature of God's covenantal relationship with us. It teaches us the way in which God desires for us to live. It teaches us the heart of relationship with Him and with all of His creatures. It teaches us how to walk before the Lord. The Bible truly is a "lamp to my feet and a light to my path."

The Bible serves as a *reproof* as well. Spending top-quality time in the Word will open up new understandings of the way in which our lives fail to measure up to God's call. The Bible is a mirror in which we can see our lives reflected. The writer to the Hebrews (in 4:12-13) noted that God's Word does not allow any denial or evasion of the truth:

> Indeed, the word of God is living and active, sharper than any two-edged sword, piercing until it divides soul from spirit, joints from marrow; it is able to judge the thoughts and intentions of the heart. And before him no creature is hidden, but all are naked and laid bare to the eyes of the one to whom we must render an account.

When Paul uses the word *correction,* he is referring to careful and sensitive redirection. As a rocket speeds through outer space, occasionally it needs midcourse corrections to keep it on its path. Similarly, the Word enables those who listen carefully to find those "midcourse corrections" that build a healthy relationship with God.

The word *training* has overtones of discipline as a result of instruction—as we train our children, they gain perspective and direction at the same time. The Bible provides both the perspective and the direction to serve God appropriately.

All this guidance is seen under the umbrella of grace. Regular time spent in the Word becomes an avenue of grace for our lives.

Bible Reading as a Means of Grace

In his sermon titled "The Means of Grace," John Wesley includes "searching the Scriptures" (which implies reading, hearing, and meditating thereon).[1] He recognizes that there is no inherent power in searching the Scriptures, for our salvation is the gift of God through Christ alone: "In using all means [of grace], seek God alone . . . Nothing short of God can satisfy your soul."[2]

Later in the sermon he writes: "All who desire the grace of God are to wait for it in searching the Scriptures."[3] He identifies several passages in support of his thesis. First, he quotes the words of our Lord himself in John 5:39: "Search the scriptures . . . it is they that testify on my behalf." He then turns to Acts 17:11-12 and comments on the number of the Bereans who believed because they "examined the scriptures every day." His third supportive text was 2 Tim. 3:15-17—a passage discussed in the previous section.

> **The Word enables those who listen carefully to find those "mid-course corrections" that build a healthy relationship with God.**

Wesley is quick to note that Scripture functions as a means of grace both for the one "who belongs to God" and the one who is still searching in the darkness. He concludes this section of the sermon with the words: "Let all, therefore, who desire that day to dawn [the one mentioned in 2 Pet. 1:19] upon their hearts, wait for it in searching the Scriptures."[4]

One of the most famous lines from John Wesley is "O give me that book! At any price, give me the book of God!"[5] His primary interest in spiritual formation is clearly visible in the preface to his *Explanatory Notes upon the Old Testament:* "It is not to draw inferences from the text, or to show what doctrines may be proved thereby . . . I design only, like the hand of a dial, to point every man to this; . . . to keep his eye fixed upon the naked Bible, that he may read and hear it with understanding."[6]

When one approaches Bible reading, not as a duty or a

discipline, but as one of God's primary ways of distributing grace to us, it drastically changes the whole picture. The hunger for God can be satisfied only by the bread of life.

BIBLE READING FOR PERSONAL GROWTH

Many persons approach the reading of the Bible as a duty. They struggle to find a system by which they can work their way through it. They deliberately cover the designated amount of material. But they fail to find nourishment in their inner beings from the process. Here are some recommendations for allowing grace to flow through your Bible reading.

1. Begin with Prayer

Wesley asserted that persons should always approach the Bible with "serious and earnest prayer."[7] He firmly believed that the Holy Spirit is as directly involved in guiding modern readers of the Bible as He was in guiding those who wrote it originally. "The Spirit of God not only inspired those who wrote it, but continually inspires, supernaturally assists, those that read it with earnest prayer."[8]

The emphasis here is upon placing ourselves in a context in which God can clearly speak to us. We recognize the crucial importance of the material we are reading. It is God's special revelation of himself to us. If there is any possibility of knowing God, it is in the Word, where He has revealed himself to us.

Wesley also recommended that each session of Bible reading "be closed with prayer, that what we read may be written on our hearts."[9] The emphasis here is upon the movement of truth from the head to the life. Intellectual knowledge of the material is not enough.

2. Set a Designated Time

The ability to really listen to the Word for personal growth requires a consistent pattern of delving into Scripture. It ought to be a time that is specifically designated for devotional reading. It is valuable to find a place where you will be unhindered in the process of reading. Uninterrupted time allows us to devour the message for our personal growth.

Wesley's own instructions were: "Set apart a little time, if you can, every morning and evening for that purpose."[10] Since spiritual growth is such a high priority in our lives, the time we designate should not be the time left over after all else is done. It is important to give top-quality time to this endeavor. When we are harried and frazzled, our attention is short and our ability to listen is reduced.

> **Persons who read the Word
> only in tiny snippets
> are far more likely to read their
> own ideas into Scripture.**

Sit in a comfortable setting and cultivate the skill of listening for the voice of the Spirit in the process of giving dedicated time to God and His Word. "The Christian's interest in Scripture has always been in hearing God speak, not in analyzing moral memos. The common practice is to nurture a listening disposition—the involving ear rather than the distancing eye—hoping to become passionate hearers of the word rather than cool readers of the page."[11]

The anticipation of a specific time alone with the Lord—even when snatched from a very busy schedule—begins to condition us to listen more skillfully. Eugene Peterson reminds us: "The Christian community came into being *listening,* not *looking.*"[12]

3. Reading with the Eyes of the Heart

In Eph. 1:17-19, Paul prays this prayer for his readers:

I pray that the God of our Lord Jesus Christ, the Father of glory, may give you a spirit of wisdom and revelation as you come to know him, so that, with the eyes of your heart enlightened, you may know what is the hope to which he has called you, what are the riches of his glorious inheritance among the saints, and what is the immeasurable greatness of his power for us who believe, according to the working of his great power.

The process of allowing "the eyes of the heart" to be opened is a special part of the working of grace. In the Early Church, books were not readily available, and everyone listened to the reading of the text. They were skilled listeners. With the advent of printing and the processes of modern education, listening has become a lost art. Walter Ong calls us "the most abject prisoners of the most literate culture."[13] Now we must learn again to listen to God in and through the Bible.

The Old Testament word "Torah" (the word for the *law* in Hebrew), included the connotation of guide and friend and instructor. To study Torah, in rabbinic terms, was to listen to God and receive instructions from a covenantal friend.

But how do we turn our eyes into ears again? When Moses gave instructions to Israel, he commanded a regular attention to the great truths—beginning with the daily repetition of "Hear, O Israel: The Lord is our God, the Lord alone." Then he charged: "Keep these words that I am commanding you today in your heart" (Deut. 6:4, 6). The Psalmist pledged: "I delight to do your will, O my God; your law is within my heart" (Ps. 40:8).

Robert Mulholland, in his book with the perceptive title *Shaped by the Word: The Power of Scripture in Spiritual Formation*, makes the helpful distinction between formational and informational reading. Informational reading is linear reading, which covers as much material as quickly as possible. The purpose is to master the text by objectifying and critiquing it. This problem-solving mentality drives us to be analytical and judgmental in order to gain as much as possible from the process.

Formational reading, on the other hand, reads in

depth to capture the dynamic of the message. Speed and coverage are not nearly as important as an openness to the mystery of God in the Word. Instead of seeking to master the text, we allow the text to master us. The approach is humble, detached, willing, and loving. It is a relational rather than a functional approach.

Robert Mulholland wrote: "We need time to slow down. We need time to let go of the controls. We need time to relax in order to be prepared in our inner spirits for formational reading. Even this preparation itself is spiritually forming."[14]

4. Pay Attention to the Whole Bible

John Wesley recommended that daily Bible reading include material from both the Old and the New Testament.[15] Wesley was a student of the whole Word of God. His writing and preaching demonstrate a knowledge of the meaning of individual passages in light of the whole Bible.

There is a strong temptation to read only those passages that have been meaningful to us in the past. There is an equally strong tendency to read only from the New Testament. To counter these tendencies, it is useful to follow a pattern that will expose us to the whole range of Scripture. God has spoken to us in the whole Word.

The by-product of such a disciplined range of reading is an overall perspective of God's message to us. I recall with great joy the year that the range of biblical truth in Handel's *Messiah* reinforced my reading from the Bible itself. The larger picture enables us to understand the individual sections much more easily. We learn to think in the context of the whole.

Persons who read the Word only in tiny snippets are far more likely to read their own ideas into Scripture. They frequently try to interpret Scripture instead of allowing Scripture to interpret them.

Wesley went on to urge that Bible reading always be done within the boundaries of theological reflection. His instructions were: "Have a constant eye to . . . the connexion and harmony there is between those grand, fundamental doctrines, original sin, justification by faith, the new birth, inward and outward holiness."[16] To be sensitive to theological connections also helps us see the grand, overall perspective of God's message to us and protects us from taking ideas out of context.

> **The Word of Scripture should never stop sounding in your ears and working in you all day long.**

5. Meditation upon the Word

The Psalmist makes frequent references to meditating upon the words of the Lord. One example is Ps. 119:15: "I will meditate on your precepts, and fix my eyes on your ways."

Dietrich Bonhoeffer, a German theologian who died in a Nazi prison camp, wrote an "Introduction to Daily Meditation." He recommended a studied focus upon the Word in order "to meet Christ in His Word. We go to the text curious to hear what He wants to let us know and to give us through His Word."[17] To dwell upon a text (of varying length, but he recommends 10 to 15 verses for a whole week) with the intention of receiving and accepting these words into your heart is meditation.

> The Word of Scripture should never stop sounding in your ears and working in you all day long, just like the words of someone you love. And just as you do not analyze the words of someone you love, but accept them as they are said to you, accept the Word of Scripture and ponder . . . this Word long in your heart until it has gone right into you and taken possession of you.[18]

At first meditation will be difficult, for we have trained ourselves to race on to the next idea. It will require disciplined effort to keep bringing our thoughts back to the same themes and ideas. Read them over and over again. Write down your thoughts and reflect upon them in your spiritual journal. Pray for the enabling of the Holy Spirit to focus upon these significant ideas. Be careful not to get impatient with yourself as you begin learning this skill.

Robert Mulholland writes of the "complex structure of habits, attitudes, and perceptions, of dynamics of personal and corporate relationship, and of patterns of reaction and response to the world"[19] by which we protect ourselves from the invasion of new truth. It is necessary for God to break through this "self-constructed facade—a crust of self"[20] in order to create spiritual growth. Contemplative meditation is one way we learn to allow God to "create in us a whole new structure of habits, attitudes, and perceptions, of dynamics of personal and corporate relationships, of patterns of reaction and response to the world."[21]

6. Faithful Reading and Faithful Living

Walter Brueggeman has written a book titled *Interpretation and Obedience*.[22] The point of the book is that there is an essential link between obedience and interpretation of Scripture. He uses terms like "interpretive obedience" and "obedient interpretation."

God offers us a new life in Christ. To respond to this stupendous offer of eternal life is a privilege. Each response to the truth revealed in the Word becomes the vestibule to a richer and deeper insight.

John Wesley's instructions in this regard called for self-examination in the process of listening to the voice of the Spirit in the Word. Then he recommended: "And whatever light you then receive should be used to the uttermost, and that immediately. Let there be no delay. Whatever you resolve, begin to execute the first moment you can. So shall you find this word to be indeed the power of God unto present and eternal salvation."[23]

Interpretation and obedience are inextricably related.

Unless we obey the truths already revealed, it is unlikely that God will bless us with additional revelation. There is an inextricable relationship between knowing and doing, between faithful reading and faithful living. The Word says, "Then Jesus said to the Jews who had believed in him, 'If you continue in my word, you are truly my disciples; and you will know the truth, and the truth will make you free'" (John 8:31-32).

The Scriptures are one instrument God uses to shower grace on waiting and obedient persons. To refuse that avenue of His grace results in an anemic and emaciated spiritual life. To strategically choose to live under that shower of grace results in a fruitful and dynamic spiritual life— one God can shape for Kingdom purposes.

▶ For Personal Reflection and Action ◀

1. Reviewing Important Concepts

A. Go back over chap. 5 and make a list of four or five Ideas or insights that are meaningful to you.

B. Reorganize the list of ideas and insights, ranking them in order of their significance to you at your present place on your spiritual journey.

C. Thinking of the two ideas or insights that top your prioritized list, consider this question: If you were to teach this chapter to an adult class, how would you present your top two insights and ideas on posters or on a bulletin board display?

2. Bible Study

A. Reread what this chapter has to say about "Reading with the Eyes of the Heart."

B. Study Paul's prayers for the Ephesians in 1:17-19 and Eph. 3:14-21. Try to let God speak to you through these texts, that is, try to read for *transformation* rather than *information*. You may wish to make the hymn "Break Thou the Bread of Life" (Hymn 693 in *Sing to the Lord*) a part of this devotional experience.

3. Create a Plan

If you are not currently engaged in regular, systematic Bible study, decide now what parts of the Bible you will begin to study. Write out your plans for Bible study at least one week in advance.

"Be joyful always; pray continually; give thanks in all circumstances, for this is God's will for you in Christ Jesus" (1 Thess. 5:16-18, NIV).

6

Meeting God in Prayer

Prayer, the core activity of the Spirit-filled life, is simple yet profound, easy to understand while inexhaustible in its truth. Prayer is an essential in the spiritual journey. There is no spiritual formation, no holy life, no growth in Christlikeness without it. The Divine Presence remains far-off, cold, and unknown without prayer. We neglect prayer to our own inner peril. "Prayer is the most encompassing experience of the spiritual life. It is as essential to the Spirit's unfolding as bread is to the body."[1]

John Wesley emphasized the priority of private prayer. Nothing could take its place. Joseph Benson, a scholar and protégé of Wesley, was reminded that the study of theology could not replace it. "Let not study," Wesley wrote to him in a letter, "swallow up . . . the hours of private prayer."[2] Not even Christian service should crowd out prayer. Wesley warned his student Ann Bolton, "Let not your works of mercy rob you of time for private prayer."[3]

WHAT IS PRAYER?

To keep prayer from becoming difficult, if not spiritually impotent, we need to understand it in its broadest sense. From that perspective, we can discuss the particulars of such a vital means of grace.

1. Prayer Is Talking with God

It is conversation with the Creator and lover of our souls. We talk to Him as we would anyone we love and trust. There is no need for affected, pious language and ponderous tones. We are conversing friend to friend, heart to heart. Prayer is interaction between God and us.

Prayer is more than a designated 15 minutes a day, as important as that may be. It is an ongoing relationship, a continual dialogue with the Heavenly Father. Prayer at this level becomes as natural as breathing, as the ancient writers regularly remind us. In this sense, our very lives become prayers.

This is not so hard to imagine. Think for a moment of the times in a day when you breathe a prayer to God. Perhaps it's a distressed friend who asks a question that has no answers, and so you lift a prayer for wisdom. Perhaps your attention is drawn to the homeless figure staggering along the sidewalk, and so you whisper a prayer for him. Breath becomes prayer.

2. Prayer Is Aligning Ourselves with the Purposes of the Divine Creator

It is agreeing with God and participating with Him in what He is about in our world. Prayer is bringing my desires, plans, hopes, and wishes in line with His creative and redeeming intent.

3. Prayer Is Change

This principle makes prayer easy and difficult at the same time. Prayer changes us as the God of the universe brings us more and more in conformity to the image of His Son. He searches out our hidden places, calling us to full disclosure and thereby renewal, healing, and change. If we intend to pray, we need to be ready to be changed.

4. Prayer Is Both Rest and Battle

Prayer is rest as we learn to be with Jesus everywhere we go, open to constant awareness and presence. In the midst of our hectic days, He promises a rest at the center of our beings.

But prayer is also battle as we engage in a frontal attack on the enemy and his strongholds. We will not be caught off guard by superficial concepts of prayer but will recognize that prayer means real spiritual struggle.

To understand prayer in such a way is to put phrases like "At least I can pray" in their proper perspective. It is not the least we can do—it is the most important thing we can do.

5. Prayer Is Linking Our Will and Spiritual Energies with God's Power

Maxie Dunnam, in *The Workbook of Intercessory Prayer*, raised a question from which I have not been able to escape. "What if there are some things God either cannot or will not do until people pray?" Could it be true that actions in the drama of life are in some way or other dependent on the intercessors backstage? There are biblical examples of such a conditional connection as in 2 Chron. 7:14 and John 15:7. As Dunnam is quick to point out, this in no way diminishes the sovereignty of God but highlights the marvelous relationship we have with God in prayer.[4]

If Dunnam is right, what changes should that make in your prayer life?

TEACH ME TO PRAY

What should be the content of our praying? Is there a framework upon which I can build my own unique way of praying? I believe there is. It is both ages-old and up-to-date. It is the ACTS pattern, the letters signifying Adoration, Confession, Thanksgiving, and Supplication.

Adoration

All our praying (except for maybe the foxhole emergency type) should begin with adoration. We start by worshiping and glorifying the God who loves us and has redeemed us. How do you adore Him? What names, titles, descriptors do you use?

When I first seriously examined my prayer patterns, I discovered that my adoration vocabulary was meager indeed. A friend helped me by suggesting I use the alphabet. Following his advice, I made a list of "adoration" descriptors, writing one word for each letter of the alphabet. Then I prayed it. What a breakthrough for me! I began to record these adoration words in my prayer journal, going back to them and adding new ones as they came to my attention.

We want God to do our bidding more than we want Him.

Many Christians find the prayer of adoration difficult. Kenneth Leech suggests that may be due to "the fact that we carry over into our prayer the utilitarian and functional notions which govern our work-based society."[5] That is to say that most of our life is governed by ideas about efficiency and production. Both people and things "are valued for their results, for what they produce."[6] But the prayer of adoration rises far above such utilitarian motivation. It is about praise and freedom, liberty and love, majesty and the glory of God. How do you reduce to piecework phrases like these?

> Joyful, joyful, we adore Thee,
> God of glory, Lord of love;
> Hearts unfold like flow'rs before Thee,
> Opening to the sun above.

Do you suppose Henry Van Dyke was being paid by the hour when he wrote that hymn?

Confession

Confession is the time I bring to the Lord the sins, failures, and needs of my life. It's not easy—but it's healthy! This is the time I get honest with God. Whatever He brings to my awareness, whatever needs the atoning blood, I surrender to Him.

How easy it is to skip confession and go straight to the "asking for" part of prayer. But confession must not be omitted.

There are several uses of confession. *One is the confession of sins.* As we open our hearts to God, the searchlight of His holiness may show us some sin that needs to be confessed and forgiven. The only proper thing to do is to confess that sin at once and receive His forgiveness. The biblical term *confess* is made by joining the word for *speak* and the word for *alike* or *agree*. Then *confession* means to *speak alike* or *speak in agreement*. When we *confess* our sins we are speaking, telling God that we agree with Him on the subject of our spiritual condition.

Remember that saved and sanctified men and women do not have to sin, but sometimes they do. And when they do, prompt confession is needed. We approach the confession part of our prayer in repentance—but in confidence as well, because we know that "if we confess our sins, he is faithful and just to forgive us our sins, and to cleanse us from all unrighteousness" (1 John 1:9, KJV).

1 John, chapters 1 and 2, deal at length with what a Christian should do when he or she strays into sin. The answer is to walk in the light and confess our sin, for if we do, the blood of Jesus Christ goes right on cleansing us from all sin.[7]

The worst thing we can do is deny our sin. If in such a situation "we say that we have no sin, we deceive ourselves" (1 John 1:8, KJV). Nothing squelches the spiritual life more quickly and completely than unconfessed sin.

Another use for confession has to do with the need for sanctifying grace. We confess our inward sin that wars against the soul. Being radical optimists about the possibilities of grace, we do believe that God can purify the sinful heart, sanctifying us "through and through" as the Scriptures repeatedly promise.

Through the ages, the saints have celebrated the purifying work of the Holy Spirit. Macarius in the fifth century wrote that just as metal that is cast into the fire is purified, "the soul that has . . . received the heavenly fire . . . is disentangled from all the love of the world, and set free from all the corruptions of the affections."[8] The diligent seeker will one day be "anointed with the sanctifying . . . oil of gladness . . . and . . . the very spirit of holiness."[9] Then "sin is rooted out and man receives the original formation of Adam in his purity."[10] Then "as a stone in the . . . sea is in every way surrounded with water; so are those cleansed by the Spirit every way drenched with the Holy Spirit and made like Christ."[11]

> **Prayer is the soaring of the human spirit to meet and be with the Spirit of God.**

Time and space do not permit citing testimonies from spiritual giants who through the ages have discovered and taught about holiness of heart and life. The Wesleyan heritage of entire sanctification and holy living rests on the strong foundation of the Holy Bible and the testimony of the saints in every age.

Let modern writer Albert E. Day say it for us all: "On this I would venture my eternal salvation—if you will make the purity of God your indefatigable quest, the God of purity will give himself to you in such fullness, that your questions will be transcended in the splendor of the experience that has overtaken you."[12]

Do you lack or desire inner purity? Confess that need in prayer.

Does the sanctified Christian, then, have nothing to confess? John Wesley taught us that "the most holy among us" have reason to use confessional prayer regularly. *The third use of confession has to do with confession in the prayers of the sanctified.*

Even "the most holy among us" are members of a fallen race, subject to a thousand infirmities. Being such, we repeatedly fall short of the mark of God's holiness. Our judgment is flawed, our reason inadequate, our knowledge deficient, and our performance of duty sometimes erratic—even though our *intention* is to do only the right.

A much-neglected teaching of Wesleyanism is that these shortcomings, infirmities, faults, and failures due to our fallenness, while not properly called sins, still need the atoning blood of Christ to make us acceptable to God. Thus "the most holy among us" must confess the need for grace to cover mistakes and failures.

Closely related to this is that we must regularly confess our need for the Spirit to keep on cleansing us from all sin. The cleansing of the Spirit is not once and for all. When we are made holy by sanctifying grace, God does not give us a lifetime supply of holiness. Rather, we are kept holy by the moment-by-moment cleansing of the blood of Jesus. John Wesley declared, "The most perfect . . . need the blood of the atonement, and may properly . . . say 'Forgive us our trespasses.'"[13] He goes on to say, "We need the power of Christ every moment . . . to continue in the spiritual life and without which, notwithstanding our present holiness, we should be devils the next moment."[14]

Thus, we see that the "C" in the ACTS formula for prayer is for every one of us.

Thanksgiving

We are now ready for thanksgiving. This is much easier for most of us, yet we seldom take time to seriously thank Him. Paul, writing to the Thessalonians, reminded them (and us), "Be joyful always; pray continually; give thanks in all circumstances, for this is God's will for you in Christ Jesus" (1 Thess. 5:16-18, NIV). To pray the ACTS pattern consistently, with careful attention to a thankful spirit, will go a long way toward enabling a winsome and healthy, Spirit-filled life-style.

Jesus himself is our example when it comes to prayers of thanksgiving. When Jesus stood with the sack lunch in His hand and 5,000 hungry people in front of Him, He did not shift into a bishop tone and pray, "Father, we need a miracle! We believe you can do it!" No, rather He simply prayed, "Thank you . . ."[15]

When He stood at the grave of His friend Lazarus He did not ask everyone to join hands and form a prayer circle and hum "I Would Not Be Denied." Rather, He prayed, "Father, I thank thee that thou hast heard me" (John 11:41, KJV).

> **When it stands before You and Your infallible Truthfulness, doesn't my soul look just like a market place where the second-hand dealers from all corners of the globe have assembled to sell the shabby riches of this world?**
> —Karl Rahner
> *Encounters with Silence*

How the *man* Jesus must have felt when He ate His "last supper" with His disciples, knowing that betrayal and death were at the door! Yet He took the bread, called it the symbol of His own broken body—and He prayed a prayer of thanks (Luke 22:19). When He took the cup filled with wine the color of His own blood, He again offered a prayer of thanks (v. 17). And He went to His death singing a hymn (Mark 14:26). We do not know the words, but who would be surprised if the hymn He sang on the way to the Cross was a song of thanksgiving?

Let us follow our Lord's pattern constantly, offering prayers of thanksgiving in all circumstances.

Supplication

The prayer of supplication embraces both petition and intercession. In this sort of prayer we ask God to meet our own needs and the needs of others for whom we pray.

When I was young, petition took first place—sometimes the only place. It took me years to take seriously the words of Jesus, "Seek ye first the kingdom of God." What we ask God for must be subject to and sanctioned by both the will of God and the good of the Kingdom. That's what Samuel Young meant when he confessed that he often prayed, "Lord, edit my prayers."

Supplication opens the door to intercession, defined as standing between two parties and pleading the case to one on behalf of the other. Of all the prayer ministries open to a Christian, this one could be considered the most singularly important, and possibly the most difficult.

Intercessory prayer includes the significant people in our lives: family, children, loved ones, friends. It can be as large a ministry as God leads and you are willing to follow, interceding for those around the country and throughout the world.

If you are sometimes confused about how to pray for others, try a personalized version of the Lord's Prayer in behalf of that person for whom you want to pray. Just fill in the blanks with that person's name.

PRAYING THE LORD'S PRAYER FOR OTHERS

_____'s Father who art in heaven
Hallowed be thy name in _____.
Thy kingdom come in _____.
Thy will be done in _____ on earth just as if he/she were with you in heaven. Give _____ this day his/her daily bread, and forgive _____

his/her trespasses as he/she forgives those who trespass against him/her.

Lead not _____ into temptation, but deliver him/her from the evil one.

Let _____'s joy be in your kingdom, your power and your glory forever. Amen.

Another tool for intercessory prayer is Psalm 23.

AN INTERCESSORY MEDITATION: USING PSALM 23

Close your eyes and picture a person you know who is going through a difficult time. Get a sense of the reality of that person—appearance, tone of voice, etc.

Then, quietly meditate on the 23rd psalm, using this person's name instead of the personal pronouns. The following translation is from the American Bible Society's *Today's English Version:*

The Lord is _____'s shepherd; _____ has everything he/she needs.

He lets _____ rest in fields of green grass and leads _____ to quiet pools of fresh water.

He gives _____ new strength.

He guides _____ in the right paths, as he has promised.

Even if he/she go[es] through deepest darkness, _____ will not be afraid, Lord, because you are with him/her.

Your shepherd's rod and staff protect _____.
You prepare a banquet for _____, where all his/her enemies can see _____;

You welcome _____ as an honored guest and fill _____'s cup to the brim.

I know that your goodness and love will be with
_____ all _____'s life; and your
house will be _____'s home as long as
he/she lives. Amen.

THE BREATH PRAYER

One final suggestion about prayer. A simple practice
has begun to find root in the soil of my daily routine. Suggested by Ron Del Bene, it is one way of praying without
ceasing.[16] He calls it "breath prayer." It is composed of two
segments comprising six to eight syllables. First is naming
God. What do you call Him? What is the worship name response that comes to mind? The second half is a response
to the question, "What do you want me to do for you?"
What would be your response; what is your need?

Begin saying your prayer as you go about your day—
when getting ready for work, doing the dishes, idling at a
stoplight, waiting in line. Let it become your ceaseless
prayer.

As an example, while writing this very chapter I began to experience writer's block. For half a day I could not
get through the wall. My breath prayer for the next day became "Creative Spirit, unblock my mind"—not a very elo-
quent prayer, but I began to pray it as I fell asleep. As I
arose the next morning, I prayed it repeatedly, slowly, in
time with my breathing. Before I sat down at the writing
table, I knew the next sentence, and that was all it took.

Another method for consistent intercession for ones
we love is based on their birth date in each month. The
birthdays in my family come on the 2nd, 21st, and 30th
days of the month. Therefore, I pray especially for my wife
and children every month on those days. As far as prayer
support goes, it gives them 12 birthdays a year. To remember, I switch a ring or watch to another hand or arm. Every
time I notice the "out of place" ring or watch during the
day, I breathe a prayer for that family member.

Intercession must be followed by obedience. You will

find that when you ask God to do something for someone on your prayer list, He will often want to use you to help bring about the answer. Intercession is risky but profitable to the obedient.

Prayer is as simple as breathing, as the ancient writers have reminded us. Whatever else we may pontificate about prayer, Susan Muto had it right when she concluded: "Prayer is many things, yet it is one. It is the soaring of the human spirit to meet and be with the Spirit of God . . . Prayer in the end is about this all consuming love relation between God and us . . . The immediate end of prayer may be to consider some mystery of Christ's life, to resolve a problem, to see guidance for a practical course of action. But the ultimate end of prayer is always communion with God."[17]

▶ For Personal Reflection and Action ◀

1. Bible Study
Study the prayers of Paul in
Phil. 1:3-11
Eph. 1:15-23
Eph. 3:14-19

2. Review the ACTS System of Prayer in This Chapter
Use it as a guide for prayer and see if it works for you.

3. Prayer Starters
John Wesley believed that when we are tired, depressed, or sick we fail to "pray as we ought." Therefore, he taught his people to use a written prayer as a starter, which would then be followed by extemporary prayer. The early Wesleyans did this in both public and private prayer.

Try starting your devotions with one of these prayers used by John Wesley and our spiritual ancestors.

(1) A Prayer for Holy Relationships
O Father of mercies, grant that I may look on the de-

fects of my neighbor as if they were my own, that I may conceal and be grieved for them; and that making Thy love to us, O blessed Jesus, the pattern of my love to them, I may above all things endeavor to promote their eternal welfare . . .

Teach me to have compassion for the weakness and frailties of my brethren; to put the best construction on all their actions; to interpret all doubtful things to their advantage, and cheerfully to bear with their real infirmities.[18]

(2) A Prayer for Purity of Heart

Almighty God, unto whom all hearts be open, all desires known, and from whom no secrets are hid; cleanse the thoughts of our hearts by the inspiration of Thy Holy Spirit, that we may perfectly love Thee, and worthily magnify Thy holy name through Christ our Lord. Amen.[19]

(3) Review the Lord's Prayer and 23rd psalm models of intercessory prayer. Look at your prayer list and pray for two persons every day this week using these models. Record this experience in your journal.

Oh my God, when will silence, retirement, and prayer become the occupations of my soul as they are now frequently the objects of my desires? How am I wearied with saying so much and yet doing so little for You! Come, Jesus, come, You the . . . center and supreme happiness of my soul!

—Thomas à Kempis
Imitation of Christ

7

Meeting God Through Blessed Subtraction

Rev. Earl Lee, pastor emeritus of the First Church of the Nazarene in Pasadena, Calif., introduced me to "blessed subtraction" as a spiritual discipline. The southern California life-style is one of "hectic addition." Most of us were in the fast lane, upwardly mobile, adding houses and lands— and second and third jobs to meet the payments on them. Pastor Lee would challenge us to subtract instead of add in order to become better Christians.

For those who are serious about living the holy life, "blessed subtraction" becomes a precious spiritual discipline. What can you give up that would help you draw closer to God? I am not talking about sins in your life; I refer to good or morally neutral things.

There are times when, under the guidance of the Spirit, we should withdraw from convivial fellowship to be alone with God and silent before Him. Sometimes we withdraw (without ado) from the table where our daily bread is served, focusing on prayer and God. At other times, we may go on a fast from the entertainments and pleasures that so many seek. We may, under the leadership of the Spirit, subtract the popular materialism that makes acquiring things look like the blessing of God.

All these things melded together produce what is often called Christian simplicity. In our journey toward wholeness or holiness we can look at the roadmaps left by 20 centuries of saintly living. Those pilgrims practiced blessed subtraction, and they hand that heritage on to us.

SOLITUDE: SUBTRACTING CONVIVIAL COMPANY

In those thumbnail sketches of Jesus' life we call the Gospels, those brief accounts in which only the highlights of Jesus' life can be treated, we find that Jesus repeatedly sought solitude. Solitude before God was a spiritual discipline so important that not even the God-Man Jesus Christ could neglect it.

We, too, must from time to time leave the good company of family and friends to be alone before God. That is, we must practice blessed subtraction by foregoing human company for solitude that only God is welcome to invade. It is the beginner as well as the mature Christian who will find solitude a way of strength on the journey.

In solitude, we get ourselves away, not primarily for relaxation or to be refreshed by nature—though that may happen. It is to be alone, to think and muse, and to know the freedom that solitude can bring.

I have found such havens of retreat on the lake, in a forest, in a secluded corner of a university library, and even in the Saturday masses of a shopping mall. All of us can find our place and time for solitude that will fit our personalities and life's situations. In spite of any benefits to solitude, and there are many, the controlling reason for this "blessed subtraction" is to meet with the risen Christ face-to-face.

Dallas Willard, after a careful review and critique of

the disciplines as they were practiced in the early monasteries, says, "Of all the disciplines of abstinence, solitude is generally the most fundamental in the beginning of the spiritual life, and it must be returned to again and again as that life develops."[1]

A friend of mine, a people-tired, frazzled Kansas pastor, had finally acquired enough frequent flyer credits to get a trip anywhere in the United States where Delta Airlines flies. He chose Anchorage, Alaska. It took five days in a small hotel overlooking the bay for him "to find his soul again."

Of course, not everyone can fly to Anchorage when the Lord beckons him or her to the retreat of solitude. And who can find five days—for anything?

We must learn to discover the "moments of solitude" that fill our days. It may take some careful observation, but they are there. What about those moments in the morning before leaving for work, or after everyone else has left? Are there spaces of time on the bus, train, or in your car?

Are there moments during the workday that can be captured for Christ? Examine your evening patterns, the family routine before and after mealtime. What time is available before retiring? The list is endless. As we desire solitude, the Holy Spirit will give us the creativity to find it.

If you have no time for solitude, you must change your life-style. For if you do not find yourself alone, you will not find yourself at all.

Solitude has much to give us, including these gifts celebrated by Henri J. Nouwen. "It is in solitude that we discover that being is more important than having, and that we are worth more than the result of our efforts. In solitude we discover that our life is not a possession to be defended, but a gift to be shared."[2]

SILENCE: Subtracting Talkativeness and Noise

Solitude and silence go together. They complete one another. The challenge of silence comes not only in the subtraction or elimination of noise, at least for a while, but also in being quiet and not speaking.

We live in a culture of noise. Radio, television, telephones, answering machines, beepers, car phones, neon signs, billboards, junk mail, all bombard us with words and noise.

We have become so used to noise that some people cannot study without a rock music background. Others can't bear not to have the television set going while doing chores or reading—even if they aren't interested in the program.

> **Don't lose your head over what perishes . . . don't mistake what you possess for what you are. Accumulating things is useless.**
> —Evelyn Underhill
> *The House of the Soul* and
> *Concerning the Inner Life*

We have become so acclimated to noise that we fear silence—even in church. Our hyperactive society leaves us without the skill or the courage to "hasten unto Him who calls you in the silences of your heart."[3]

Not only do we neglect silence, but some work hard to avoid it. "We . . . seek to escape silence [because] . . . it evokes nameless misgivings, guilt feelings, strange, disquieting anxiety."[4] If, however, we can conquer our fear of silence, "we may experience a gradual waning of inner chaos."[5]

Henri Nouwen counsels us, "Silence is the discipline by which the inner fire of God is tended and kept alive."[6]

Silence can be a way of prayer. Some people spend all their prayer time talking. Try letting silence before God lift its own wordless prayer. There are times when silence as prayer wordlessly "pleads for forgiveness or acceptance; times when our wordlessness is gratitude or adoration . . .

Sometimes silence makes us appreciate the daring with which we say 'Father' to God . . . 'Father' sometimes becomes the only word silence allows as we express inexpressibly all we feel and want and reach for."[7]

In a world headed toward information overload, disintegration of families, and more and more noise, silence is crucial to spiritual survival. Susan Muto, in her book *Pathways of Spiritual Living*, points out the following benefits of silence: It enables and facilitates bodily relaxation, sharpens the mind's attentive capabilities, it provides for worthwhile and grace-giving speech, points us toward thoughtful action, enables us to be in touch with the Holy Spirit, and finally it is preparation for His coming and preparation for hearing His voice.[8]

How, then, do we go about practicing this "means of grace" in our busy worlds? Here is a checklist of questions that might help you focus your search for answers.

1. Have you searched your life-style for places and times where silence can be created?

2. Have you listed pockets of silence in your work arena?

3. Have you made any progress in breaking your addiction to television, telephones, radio, and stereo?

4. What initiative have you taken to create specific times, places, and rituals for privacy and solitude?

5. Are you aware of the silent presence of God in any personal way at all?[9]

FASTING: SUBTRACTING FOOD FOR THE BODY; ADDING FOOD FOR THE SOUL

Whatever happened to fasting? Growing up in the church, I was always aware of "prayer and fasting." We hear a lot about giving but little about fasting. Yet, there is at least as much said in the Bible about fasting as about giving. Could it be, as Richard Foster suggests, that for our culture, fasting calls for a much more significant sacrifice than giving?

It may be that fasting has taken a backseat because it reminds us of the excessive practices of the Middle Ages. Or it could be that we have been so programmed toward consumerism and the joys of eating that for someone to call a fast unsettles us. We are concerned for his or her health and strength. How confused we are about this powerful means of grace!

Fasting always centers on God. It is not to be equated with hunger strikes or dietary fasting for losing weight. The motive is all-important. Fasting is not undertaken to manipulate God or to trigger a miracle or solve a problem. It is to deliberately say no to food in order to give attention to God. Sounds strange in the space age, doesn't it? Maybe that's a compelling reason to bring this discipline back into our lives.

Throughout the Scriptures we see that in ancient times godly persons joined prayer and fasting together. Among those biblical characters for whom fasting was important we find Moses, Elijah, David, Zechariah, Daniel, Jonah, Joel, Paul, Barnabas, Nehemiah and Isaiah.

Jesus fasted often and indicated that He expected His disciples to deny themselves and practice fasting. John Wesley called fasting "a precious means . . . which God himself has ordained . . . therefore, when it is duly used, He will give us His blessing."[10] He advised, "And with fasting let us always join fervent prayer, pouring out our whole souls before God, confessing our sins . . . humbling ourselves under his mighty hand, laying open before Him all our wants, all our quietness and helplessness."[11]

Fasting, Wesley taught, should have as its aim the glory of God. "We fast to express our sorrow and shame for . . . transgressions; to wait for an increase in purifying grace, . . . to add . . . earnestness to our prayers . . . to avert the wrath of God, and to obtain all the . . . promises . . . made . . . in Jesus Christ."[12]

It is clear that today's traveler on the highway of holiness should not ignore this personal resource for the journey. Fasting is not a coin for the cosmic vending machine that makes God "pay off." But as you practice fasting, expect gracious serendipities from God.

SUBTRACTING PLEASURES AND ENTERTAINMENTS

Today, North American culture is almost totally distracted in the greedy pursuit of pleasures, diversions, and entertainment. For example, most every Christian I know watches too much television. A pastor friend of mine fasted television for the month of March. "It was the greatest month of the year," he said. "I'm going to make it an annual event—even though my family chooses not to join me."

A colleague of mine drives 20 miles to and from work every day. She always listened to a certain radio station for that 35-minute drive each morning. One day I asked her if she had heard a certain song on that station. "No," she replied, "the Lord has been speaking to me about listening to country music. I love country music, but 70 minutes of it a day filled my mind and heart with the wrong sort of things. So now I hum a few hymns and pray stoplight prayers on the way to work."

If you are interested in the holy life, you must discipline yourself and let the Lord monitor your entertainment. All our pleasures, diversions, and entertainments are subject to "blessed subtractions" when the Spirit nudges us in that direction.

SUBTRACTING ACQUISITIVENESS

"I believe in God and everything," Larry said, "and I would like to be a better Christian. But this going to church all the time and Bible study groups and all that other stuff . . . well, it's more than I have time for. Man, I work day and night just to keep up."

I wondered whom Larry was trying to keep up with. We leaned against his 32-foot sailboat as we talked. His son drove by on the riding lawnmower and drowned out our conversation. Then we were interrupted by a another son who was tired of taking the Chevy to his golf lessons—he wanted to drive the Lincoln. We went inside so I could speak to Janet, his wife. She yelled at her daughter to turn off the 45-inch television set as she squeezed past us. She, a real estate agent, was off to an open house. The telephone rang. It was the car dealership—the R.V. camper was fixed and ready to be picked up.

I was one discouraged Sunday School teacher as I went on my way, knowing that the "keep up with the Joneses" acquisitiveness had captured Larry and Janet, body and soul. Sometimes I think we really do live by the rule that "the one with the most toys when he dies wins."

> **Where there is simplicity there is no artificiality. One does not try to appear younger, or wiser, or richer than one is—or more saintly!**
> —Albert E. Day
> *Discipline and Discovery*

I am not opposed to prosperity. I am in favor of hard work and achievement. I am also aware that the urge to acquire is the besetting sin of this age. I am also aware that I don't know any spiritual giants, any models of the deeper spiritual life who go out and buy every gadget they can make a down payment on.

I'm quite sure Maxie Dunnam was right when he said that the religion of sinners in this age is "upward mobility." Do not be surprised if, as you walk closer and closer to God, He confronts you with challenges about why you need a bigger house, a new car, a hot tub, a camcorder—or even a steak when a hamburger would do. And do not be surprised that, as you obey Him, you lose interest in impressing the neighbors, driving fancy cars, or keeping up with the Joneses.

The first step toward Christian simplicity is yielding

our compulsive acquisitiveness to the "subtracting" Lordship of Christ.

CHRISTIAN SIMPLICITY

Incorporating the various dimensions of "blessed subtraction" to our lives is to discover Christian simplicity. Subtract busyness and add solitude; subtract noise and talkativeness and add silence; subtract body food and add spiritual food; subtract pleasures and entertainment and add reflection and meditation; subtract materialistic greed and add simplicity—and you have learned to speak with Paul about contentment. "I have learned in whatever state I am, to be content: I know how to be abased, and I know how to abound. Everywhere and in all things I have learned both to be full and to be hungry, both to abound and to suffer need. I can do all things through Christ who strengthens me" (Phil. 4:11-13, NKJV).

"'Tis a gift to be simple, 'Tis a gift to be free" says an old Shaker song. Those who have discovered Christian simplicity know what the song is about. Christian simplicity reflects an inner wisdom and a comfort with the wholeness of life that is bred in solitude and expressed through certain spontaneity and joyousness [13]

Our culture measures our worth by how much we acquire and by how busy we are. If the investments are prospering and the calendar crowded, then we must be important people. But if we ever hope to develop our spiritual lives, we must find a way to make Jesus' teaching about not being overanxious about food, clothes, and stature a reality in our lives. Les L. Steele defines Christian simplicity as "a willingness to disentangle ourselves from too many commitments, relieve ourselves of debts and obligations that keep us anxious and burdened." [14]

▶ For Personal Reflection and Action ◀

1. Blessed Subtractions

Which aspects of blessed subtractions that are treated in this book are most needed in your life right now?

A. Solitude   **D.** Subtracting pleasures and
B. Silence   entertainments
C. Fasting   **E.** Subtracting acquisitiveness

2. "Subtraction" Problem

Is there a "subtraction" problem or need in your life not included in this chapter? If so, add it to the list.

3. A Game of "Make It Go Away"

(1) What would you have to make "go away" if you were to subtract acquisitiveness? A second job? Club meetings? A computer course?

(2) If the lack of solitude and silence are making your spiritual life suffer, what would you have to make "go away" in order to find solitude and silence?

(3) If pleasures and entertainment are devouring your time, energy, and money, name one thing you could do as a first step to "make it go away."

4. Follow the Spirit's Lead

It is not recommended that you try "blessed subtraction" as a sort of novel Christian experiment. Rather, pursue it only as the Spirit leads you. Give it prayerful consideration. Do not feel obigated to imitate the subtractions God has ordained for others.

5. One Size Does Not Fit All

If you have found a certain subtraction "blessed," don't try to force it on others. The worst thing we could do would be to codify and standardize "blessed subtraction." Just because the Lord led one woman to stop listening to country music on the way to work for her own spiritual welfare does not mean that such an act is what everyone else needs right now. And what if the pastor who "fasts" a month of television every year demanded that all the church members do the same thing?

The Spirit knows what you need and what others need. He will lead the openhearted to the proper "blessed subtractions." So purpose now to keep your subtractions to yourself.

6. **Bible Study**
   A. Read Phil. 4:8-20.
   B. Relate vv. 8-9 to the theme of "blessed subtraction."
   C. Reflect on vv. 10-20 as the secret of contentment, of Christian simplicity. Include "I'd Rather Have Jesus" (Hymn 456 in *Sing to the Lord*) in your Bible study devotions.

7. **Make This Prayer Your Own**

Oh, my God, when will silence, retirement, and prayer become the occupations of my soul as they are now frequently the objects of my desires? How am I wearied with saying so much and yet doing so little for You! Come, Jesus, come, You the . . . center and supreme happiness of my soul!

—Thomas à Kempis

One particular voice speaks out that is unlike any other voice because it speaks so directly to the deepest privacy and longing and weariness of each of us that there are times when the centuries are blown away like mist, and it is as if we stand with no shelter of time at all between ourselves and the one who speaks our secret name. "Come," the voice says, "unto me. All ye. Every last one."

—Frederick Buechner

A Room Called Remember

8

Meeting God Through Spiritual Reading and Meditation

Jesus promised.

He promised, "If anyone loves Me, he will keep My word; and My Father will love him, and We will come to him and make Our home with him" (John 14:23, NKJV).

How can that happen? How does it happen?

Through the ages, Christians have found that one of the ways this promise is fulfilled is through *spiritual reading. Lectio divina,* as spiritual reading is sometimes called, is reading the sacred texts in a quest for God. In ancient times, reading was not usually a silent exercise for the mind and eye. Books were rare, handmade, and expensive. They were treasures to be read aloud in those oral societies. Words were for proclaiming and hearing. The holy writings were for the mouth and the ear as well as for the mind and the eye.

"Thus the consoling word, the arresting phrase, the sentence that challenges us to the core, is repeated over and over again and, consigned to memory, remains forever available."[1] In this way, God comes to us and makes His home in us. His Word is hidden in our hearts, His home. The promise is fulfilled.

This reading for holiness, as Robin Maas calls it, is not ordinary reading. Our culture teaches us to study, analyze, exegete, and synthesize. This is reading for information. In the case of reading for leisure, we skim and speed-read. Holy reading is not reading done for some practical purpose like sermon preparation, or to learn more about the Bible, or some spiritual self-help project. *Lectio divina* is a "disciplined form of devotion, and not a method of Bible study. It is done purely and simply to come to know God to be brought before His Word, to listen."[2]

When it comes to spiritual reading, you don't rush to finish the book or chapter, or even a paragraph. Quantity is not the issue, but quality. You may read a long passage or only a sentence. Information is not the goal—encounter with God is what matters. Spiritual reading is generally associated with the Scriptures, but the same approach can be used with Christian devotional classics or any quality material that is uplifting to the soul and apt to sharpen your awareness of God's presence.

To engage in spiritual reading is in no way to minimize or shun the necessary study of other kinds. It is to say that involvement in Bible study or a Bible study group, worthy as it is, more than likely is not the same as spiritual reading. Formative reading calls for a different perspective. Rather than tackling the text, I'm letting it tackle me!

As defined by Susan Muto, "Formative reading challenges us to listen with docility to spiritual directives found in texts of lasting value. We temper the busy train of thoughts that rush through our working day in order to dwell with texts that arouse our longing for God. Such reading, done in a slowed-down way on a regular basis, re-establishes our commitment to Christ while helping us to let go of peripheral concerns."[3]

This kind of reading may be risky. No longer controlling the material, I may find God challenging me at new depths, surprising me with new truth or leading me into joy and wonder. Though such risk may cause me uneasiness or a sense of discomfort, the journey is safe in the Holy Spirit.

How Do I Get Started?

How, then, do I begin spiritual reading? Over the centuries, various methodologies have been suggested. You may have been doing something of this sort without knowing what it was. With slight variations, they contain the same basic elements.

I begin by finding a place where it is easy for me to become quiet, collected, and open to God. Spiritual reading is not done in a rush or on the run. I will need to slow down if I hope to hear what God has to say to me from the reading.

The next step is to read the text, whether Scripture or some other literature of devotional value, in an unhurried manner. The goal is not to get "through the book," but to read until I am captured by a word, phrase, or thought. It may take a chapter, or it may happen in the first verse. It doesn't matter.

For example, recently I began reading the Gospel of John. In chapter 1, verse 14, for the first time in my life, I was struck by the phrase "and we beheld His glory." I read no further. I was being encountered by the Word, and I knew it.

The third step is to let the word or passage sink into your heart. Examine it, mull over it, talk to God about it.

When the phrase from John came alive to me, I began to ask such questions as "What does glory mean? What was *His* glory? In what way do I behold His glory in my life?" Be ready to let God speak to your heart.

SPIRITUAL READING LEADS TO THE PRAYER OF MEDITATION

Spiritual reading naturally leads to meditation. It is the normal response to a reading that has caught our attention and touched our hearts. I lift my eyes from the page and meditate on its meaning, listening for God's direction. Spiritual reading is "prayer that begins as a *dialogue* and ends up as a *duet*."[4]

> **We become servants rather than masters of the word.**
> —Susan Muto
> *Pathways of Spiritual Living*

This graceful movement from reading to meditation illuminates the major difference between the Christian practice and Eastern forms. Christian meditation is based on Scripture. It is not new. That it is so little known and practiced in the Church today is the tragedy. Equating it with the modern-day versions of yoga, transcendental meditation, and cultism is like comparing apples to oranges. There are some similar characteristics, but they are basically and fundamentally different.

Christian meditation begins and majors on meditation of the Scriptures. Other sources may also be used from time to time, such as spiritual readings, nature, and life's experiences. However, the Scriptures remain the foundation. Eastern forms of meditation, in one way or another, lead to the emptying of the mind and stress ethereal detachment from the world. It is a movement away from life, a loss of identity, and an attempt to be released from this existence.

Christian meditation, to the contrary, seeks to fill the mind and heart with the wisdom and presence of God. It deepens our identity in Christ and increases our awareness of who we are in Him. It sensitizes us not only to the beauty of our world but also to its ugliness, injustices, and hurts. We are called into engagement as lights in a dark world. As Susan Muto expresses it, "Meditation enhances our understanding of life. It teaches us to carry on in compassion."[5]

Meditation, in short, is the listening side of prayer. It is stilling the noisy interior and focusing on God's loving response and guidance. The goal is not to figure out the theological problem on the textual word construction but to pause in awesome wonder and humility before the divine mystery—and to listen.

J. I. Packer calls meditation "an activity of holy thought, consciously performed in the presence of God, under the eye of God, by the help of God; as a means of communion with God . . . to let His truth make its full . . . impact on one's mind and heart."[6]

How, then, do we meditate? There are far too many methods to cover in these short pages, but here are some beginning steps.

After selecting the passage to be used, take time to read it slowly and completely. The next step is to read it again, several times if necessary, looking for a focus such as a word or theme. Stay with the focus for as long as you deem necessary. Mull it over, look at it from many angles, and listen for what God wants to say to you.

It is here that a journal is helpful. Jot down what comes to you. For meditation leads to life response. It brings a deepening that calls for involvement with our world, life changes, and serious accountability.

Let's talk about an important problem. In our modern American culture, with its emphasis on frenetic activity and full calendar schedules, is it possible to take the meditative mind-set into our daily routines?

For example, where is the working mother of small

children to find time to meditate? (Even though there are Christian masters in this spiritual discipline, they are the first to say it is for everyone. There are no secrets, no higher levels of knowledge or accomplishment. We are all beginners, and the simple fact remains that we learn to meditate by meditating.)

Back to the overscheduled working mother: can she not find meditative moments interwoven in her busy days? What about the minutes between appointments, the quiet lunch alone, those islands of silence in our day that we so easily overlook? Our automobiles, as Susan Muto suggests, can be our hermit caves, so to speak. If I am paying attention to careful driving and refuse to get caught up in the games of "Who can be first?" and "How dare you cut me off?" I find it a rewarding time of practicing His presence.

> **Meditation is simple and natural, like a seed growing and becoming a tree. At the same time it requires the right conditions, conditions not provided by the secular world today.**

At a stoplight, I intentionally observe my surroundings, focus on how good it is to be alive, or pray for my family. As the miles slip by unnoticed, I talk with God about major issues in my life. By turning off the radio and using cassette tapes I have designed for the purpose, my daily travel can be a blessed time of meditation indeed.

The results of this way of life are worth the journey. It will provide the psychological and physical benefits of other forms of meditation, but much, much more. Though we may stumble at first, the skill of meditation grows and matures as any other skill faithfully practiced. It is a way of life, not something that is constructed and forgotten, like a swing set.

Is meditation optional for the traveler on the highway of holiness? I think it is required, and I must try to provide a life climate in which spiritual reading and meditation can grow.

Morton Kelsey compares the growing seed and the soil in which it grows to the development of the art of meditation in the spiritual life. He points out that the giant redwoods started with a seed. "From one seed is grown enough wood to frame several hundred houses."[7] The soul, Kelsey notes, has that kind of potential—if the environment is right. He points out another aspect of the analogy. "Remember that only in a few mountain valleys were the conditions right for the Sequoia gigantea, the mighty redwood, to grow."[8]

Meditation is something like that. It is "simple and natural, like a seed growing and becoming a tree. At the same time it requires the right conditions, conditions not provided by the secular world today."[9]

Learn the art of meditation. Give your soul a chance to grow.

As the material we meditate on becomes integrated into our lives, we will find ourselves growing in Christlikeness. We will find ourselves thinking, imagining, and deciding on an ever-widening and deepening base of spiritual understanding and wisdom. We will be able to listen to God with more precision. We will be better able to touch a hurting world and show it the presence of a loving, healing God.

One wonderful source of meditative reading is the hymnal. Formative ideas are captured in rhythmic patterns that aid meditation. Familiar hymn tunes aid the flow of the ideas into our inner beings.

Don't worry about whether you can measure up to others in meditation skills. Just start—today. Let the Holy Spirit guide you on how to begin. Start with the Bible and a journal to capture your thoughts.

▶ For Personal Action and Reflection ◀

1. Set a definite day and time to begin with spiritual reading and meditation.

2. Find a secluded spot or room. Quiet yourself before the Lord.

3. Read the "kenosis hymn," the passage about Jesus "emptying himself of all but love" in order to bring about our salvation—Phil. 2:5-11.

4. Read the passage slowly, savor it, taste it, receive it into your heart.

5. Surrender yourself to Christ. Spiritual reading is an act of surrender to His word. You are not trying to master the text—you are seeking to be mastered by it.

A journal helps you to see if you are still on the Way
or sidetracked somewhere in some pleasant spot
that has you deceived.
—Robert Wood
A Thirty-Day Experiment in Prayer

9

Meeting God Through Journaling

The discovery of journaling as a spiritual discipline in recent years has introduced a serendipitous dimension of *hilaritas*, of cheerfulness, into the holy life-style. It also has helped Christians keep their lives focused on the things that matter most. The journaling Christian will not measure out life in coffee spoons nor fritter away his or her best energies "meandering over fields of withered fantasies and everydayness."[1]

"But not one verse in the Bible tells us to keep a journal," a brash young woman stood up and blurted out in objection.

The seminar leader reeled and tried to find something to say. But before he could recover, a middle-aged gentlemen turned smiling to the bristling objector. "True, my dear," he said, "but the Bible itself is a journal."

He was pretty close to right, I think. The Gospels are the journaled remembrances of the "four evangelists." Many of the psalms are like poetic journal entries of David's conversations with God about sin and salvation,

115

law and love, failure and faith. Paul's Epistles often sound like journals of shared adversity and mutual encouragement. The churches were permitted in these letters to look over Paul's shoulders and right into his heart as he recorded the pathos, agony, and joy of Christian service.

Journaling is not new. It has been practiced throughout the ages. Journaling is particularly at home in the Wesleyan spiritual tradition. John Wesley kept a journal that is still being reprinted in these days. Further, he urged (almost required) all his preachers and lay leaders to keep a journal. The era of the Wesleyan revival is one of the best recorded and most studied in church history. One reason for that is the journals of Methodists small and great, which are still available.

> **The complexities of life seem more simple, the storms of life more calm when they are written in our prayer journal and offered to our Lord.**

Journaling is not a requirement like prayer is. After all, there will be nonjournalers in heaven. For a few people it doesn't work very well. Some object to it—usually for unworthy reasons. "I just don't have time," some say as they punch the remote control to watch a television soap opera. Some fear that others, perhaps even family members, will read their journals and find out things that were never intended to be public knowledge. But the privacy problem can be solved easily enough.

Probe the person who resists journaling and many times the problem is fear of facing themselves honestly. "Lust is the overpowering problem of my life," one such man confessed. "I hate myself, and I try to keep that out of my mind. The last thing I need is to have to put my humiliating temptations in writing every day." Of course, if this struggling believer is ever going to find victory over his besetting sin, he must face it—not forget it. Perhaps journaling would be the spiritual discipline that would help him put himself openly in the presence of God the Deliverer.

WHY SHOULD I KEEP A SPIRITUAL JOURNAL?

Christian journaling eagerly beckons us to a generous benefits package. Here is my catalog of journaling benefits.

1. The primary benefit, which outweighs everything else in this list, is that **journaling can foster an ever-deepening relationship with God.**

2. **The journal provides a way of recording the major turning points in our lives.** It provides a way of discovering the patterns in our lives, both constructive and destructive. Having collected sufficient material, we now have the data that will help us reflect on where our life is going. It will help us pinpoint the habits and patterns that have eluded our attention. We will be able to rejoice in the positive ways God is working and provide midcourse correction for the negative patterns that appear.

3. **The journal provides a method of recording our own unique life histories.** Your journey on this earth is unique; it is like no other. In your journal, you will be able to capture your life's characteristics, movements, successes, and failures. The journal becomes your own, distinctive drama. No one else will pass this way but you. Now the journal becomes a friend, not a tyrant!

4. **The journal is a way to self-discovery and self-understanding.** How growth-producing it is when we discover as we write a new truth about ourselves! It is common for journal writers to be caught by surprise, to exclaim, "I didn't know I was like that!" or "I was totally unaware I was doing that till I wrote it down." Be prepared for deepening insights and growing self-awareness, which lead to a maturing awareness of God.

5. **The journal can be a tool for survival, a life raft in life's storms.** When we can go to no one else, we can go to our journals. There we can tell it like it is, write our situa-

tions and our responses to them. When troubles, complexities, and confusions are written, they tend to lose their overwhelming power. Now on paper, instead of swirling endlessly around in our minds like storm-tossed seas, our thoughts and imaginations are objectified, in black and white. Somehow, they are not so frightening and we are able to deal with them.

6. **Writing in a journal can provide the means for decision-making and goal-setting.** I remember several years ago when I was faced with a major change in my career. Finding an isolated third-floor corner of a university library, I worked out my thinking and decisions in my journal. To this day, when doubts arise, I can go back to that four-hour "talk" with my journal, read those entries, and walk back into that experience. Doubt flees, and I am reassured!

7. **The journal can be a form of prayer.** People learning to journal will often remark, "This is like praying." And so it is. While writing in a section, there have been times when I have moved right into a prayer with the Lord. It was so natural, so right. Some have written letters to the Lord. As our journal writing begins to touch the deep areas of our spiritual lives, it *is* prayer. It is contact and conversation with the risen Christ within.

8. **The journal creates a record of your growing, sacred love affair with God.** What joy, in reading back over that record, to discover God has been at work! Our faith is strengthened as we read and observe that we are *not* the same. The days of our lives seem to pass by without distinction, with such sameness. But our journal tells us differently. God has been here, there, in those mundane activities and ceaseless days, and we are truly being made whole!

WHAT GOES INTO A JOURNAL

Here are some guidelines for creating and using a spiritual life journal.

1. Keep it simple.
2. Begin gently, without pressure to conform or imi-

tate anyone else. What comes naturally to you is what is important.

3. Get in the habit of dating, timing, and locating each page of your journal. This helps in later reflection and in replacing a lost page.

4. Remember that a journal is something like a diary, but one that regularly records not only data but emotions, impressions, intuitions, and interpretations.

5. Stick with it—determine to give faithful attention to your journal for at least six months. By that time, benefits can begin to be "harvested." At least your basic life patterns can be discerned by that time.

6. Use your journal to build a prayer list or prayer journal. Here is an ongoing dynamic record of prayer needs, when they were first entered, and when and how they were answered. What a lift to faith to go back over the lists several months and years later!

7. One section can also contain written prayers. There are times when I must put down on paper what is going on in my heart.

8. Another section of your journal might contain scriptural insights. During your devotional reading of the Scriptures, keep your journal close at hand. After dating the page, recording the time of day and the location where you are writing (office, den, library, plane), enter any thoughts, insights, and/or questions that come from your reading. What meanings have made themselves clear to you? What is God saying to you in this passage? The possibilities are endless, and these captured gems from God's Word become priceless.

9. Another journal section might contain entries concerning significant events of life. Here you could collect, remember, and reflect upon such events as weddings, births, funerals, commencements, significant achievements, etc.

10. Other sections might be devoted to such things as conversations with God, a record of creative hunches and ideas, and a confessional page.

A MORE STRUCTURED APPROACH FOR BEGINNERS

If your personality needs more specific structure than that presented in the foregoing section, you might like the following plan.

Try to plan a 20-minute period in the evening for journaling. Before you write anything, march your whole day past your memory's review stand. Pick out significant encounters, ideas, events—pleasant or unpleasant—that give "aroma" to your memory of the day.

Now you are ready to write. Think in symbolic and poetic language. (OK, you're not a writer—but do the best you can.) Try to capture thoughts and feelings. Describe the events in graphic detail. Just tell the story of these selected events.

> **Journaling helps us to see how straight God writes in the crooked lines of life.**

Step two is to reflect on and interpret the events or insights of the day. Relate the specific experiences or the broader basic and timeless truths that stand behind them. If, for example, an experience of suffering dominated your day, you might choose to relate it to the redemptive nature of suffering and to the suffering that made salvation possible. One man, forced into early retirement by plotting colleagues, wrote in his journal, "At least they have not taken me out and crucified me like they did my Lord." This helped him get a better perspective on his own misfortunes.

Robert Wood suggests responding to these "day review" questions to get one's journal juices flowing.

What moments did you feel closest to Christ?

What moment during the day did you feel you were responding to God's call to be His disciple?

Where did you participate in "being the church" today?

When was your faith tested through failure or success today?

What is your plan for tomorrow to improve your discipleship to Christ?[2]

Choose the type of book for your journal that appeals to you. Some use nicely bound books with blank pages, others a simple spiral notebook. I prefer the smaller three-ring notebook. It is easy to create the section dividers I need, pages can be taken in and out for ease of reading and harvesting the material, and it's small enough to take with me on trips.

Keep in mind that you are not writing for a grade—you are writing for yourself and for God. Try journaling for at least six months. You'll find it well worth the effort. You might discover in it all that Susan Muto finds:

It becomes an entrance into the universal quest for spiritual meaning. It fosters a playful, hope-filled approach to living. Far from being a harsh discipline, journal-keeping becomes a condition for the possibility of free, creative, self-expression, bringing us into communion with the Personhood of God. It makes explicit the ways He has been working in our life. We feel the power and gentleness of the Lord in the gifted nature of these events. The written word evokes our consent to His plan, a yes freely given because journaling helps us to see more clearly how straight He writes in the crooked lines of life.[3]

▶ For Personal Reflection and Action ◀

1. Bible Study

A. Read Phil. 1:1-11 at least twice

B. Note the "feeling" words and phrases. Here are some of them: "thanks," "joy," "fellowship," "I have you in my heart," "I long for you with . . . affection." There are several more. Look them up and list them.

C. If you are like most people, you think of Paul as a

tough-minded missionary. We would not have known the deep love he felt for his Christian friends if he had not written to them.

D. When the Philippians read these words, what do you think they *felt, thought,* and *did?*

2. Starting a Journal

A. If you do not already keep a journal, start one today. Use whatever form you like after considering the ideas in this chapter.

B. If you prefer a structured approach, try this one:

Divide a two-page spread in your journal into five sections.

1. My spiritual life
2. My relational life
3. My intellectual life
4. My physical life
5. My life of Christian service

In the section for "spiritual life" note any aspects of your devotions, church attendance, prayer life that were meaningful—or that were barren—during the previous 24 hours.

In the "relational life" space bring forward any problems or progress in your family, marriage, school, or vocational relationships. Present them all to the Lord.

In the space labeled "intellectual life," note important things you learned from your study of the Bible. Growing Christians are always studying the Bible, right? Insights from other study, secular or sacred, can also be recorded here.

In the "physical life" category record your thoughts about exercise, recreation, health, and illness—and God's interest or relationship to them.

In the space marked "Christian service," note the ways in which you witnessed for Christ and served Him and the people for whom He died.

The Creator's children come in an infinite variety. Given this, what does spiritual formation look like in different personalities?

10

Meeting God Through Our Own Uniqueness

"As a father has compassion for his children, so the Lord has compassion for those who fear him. For he knows how we were made; he remembers that we are dust" (Ps. 103:13-14).

The Psalmist was keenly aware that God understands our fragility. He does not deal with us as automatons or robots—everyone exactly the same. God does not use a cookie cutter to create human beings—a thousand replicas in a row.

OUR CREATOR LOVES VARIETY

Annie Dillard, a scientist in love with nature, has written a fascinating little book called *Pilgrim at Tinker Creek*. She celebrates the intricacy and variety of the world of nature the Creator has given to us. She invites the reader to become intimately involved in observing these marvelous gifts: "We see a shred of the infinite possible combination of an infinite variety of forms . . . This, then, is the extravagant landscape of the world, given, given with pizzazz, given in good measure, pressed down, shaken together, and running over."[1]

The Creator's children also come in an infinite variety.

I stood on a street corner in Winnipeg, Man., a few years ago and marveled at the variety of persons God has created. The variety and range of students who have come through my classrooms in this last quarter of a century only serve to reinforce the concept. Multifaceted and variegated, indeed, are the creatures God has placed within this world.

VARIETY AND SPIRITUAL FORMATION

Given this wide and pulsating variety, what does spiritual formation look like? How does grace function in different personalities and in different cultures? When the Father has compassion on His children, how is that compassion different from person to person?

As we have seen, all of spiritual formation is a function of the grace God has granted to us. Second, as the first chapter pointed out, the essence of spiritual formation is a growing relationship with God.

Just as no two persons are exactly alike, so no two relationships are identical. The fact that relationships vary and persons differ suggests that the means of grace will function differently for differing personality types. At an international conference on personality differentiation, keynote speaker Morton Kelsey estimated that 80 percent of the books on disciplines for the spiritual life are written by 20 percent of the personality styles. Granted that it was an overstatement for effect, it does capture the point that the disciplines in the spiritual life must be keyed to the personality differences.

Remember that the disciplines in and of themselves do not create growth. Spiritual disciplines are useful methods by which to nurture our relationship with God.

Dallas Willard writes: "A discipline for the spiritual life is, when the dust of history is blown away, nothing but an activity undertaken to bring us into more effective cooperation with Christ and his Kingdom . . . Spiritual disciplines . . . are only activities undertaken to make us capable of receiving more of his life and power without harm to ourselves or others."[2]

Whenever someone comes to us for spiritual guidance, we are tempted to guide him or her to whatever particular discipline is currently providing nurture for us. We assume that everyone functions just as we do. Such an assumption deprives others of access to the ways in which God's grace may touch their lives.

The same truth functions in worship styles. When worship patterns cater to a single personality style (often the style of the one who creates the order of service), a majority of persons are less than edified. When I learned that my personality pattern appears only in 5 percent of the general population, I came to see the pattern of worship that best met my needs was frustrating to an overwhelming majority.

> **Spiritual disciplines . . . are only
> activities undertaken to make
> us capable of receiving more
> of His life and power.**

A conference on personality and worship preferences emphasized this point. Each of the 60 participants (ranging from Catholic to Quaker) had taken the Myers-Briggs personality indicator. Each conferee identified his or her personality preference on a 3" x 5" card. We were asked to write the four letters describing our particular personality type. On the opposite side we listed four of our favorite hymns. The leaders sorted the cards according to the personality type. Then, before he turned them over, he predicted our favorite hymns with 70 percent accuracy. We were all astounded—even our variety was predictable.

VARIETY AND THE BODY OF CHRIST

When Paul was writing to the Corinthians, he understood that God was the organizing center for this diverse group. Think with me about the meaning of 1 Cor. 12:4-12 (RSV) in light of spiritual formation:

Now there are varieties of gifts, but the same Spirit; and there are varieties of service, but the same Lord; and there are varieties of working, but it is the same God who inspires them all in every one. To each is given the manifestation of the Spirit for the common good. To one is given through the Spirit the utterance of wisdom, and to another the utterance of knowledge according to the same Spirit, to another faith by the same Spirit, to another gifts of healing by the one Spirit, to another the working of miracles, to another prophecy, to another the ability to distinguish between spirits, to another various kinds of tongues, to another the interpretation of tongues. All these are inspired by one and the same Spirit, who apportions to each one individually as he wills. For just as the body is one and has many members, and all the members of the body, though many, are one body, so it is with Christ.

Consider the way in which diversity relates to spiritual formation. The richness in the life of the Body of Christ is the diversity of personality and background and heredity and environment. It is no surprise, then, that the disciplines of the spiritual life function in different ways for different personality types—and even differently for the same personality type at different stages in life.

The same God whose synthesizing and coordinating skills make the body into one is the God who graces the relationships we recognize as spiritual formation. The same Spirit who coordinates the Body of Christ is the Spirit who shepherds individuals in spiritual development. Thanks be to God for His marvelous variety! He really does have pizzazz.

Personality Style as a Key to the Means of Grace

Many different instruments are available to help understand the effect of personality preference upon the functioning of the means of grace. One example is the Myers-Briggs Temperamant Indicator (commonly known as the MBTI)[3], which is used to discuss the role of personality type in areas as diverse as educational style, leadership style, marriage choice, and many others.

In the next few pages the categories of MBTI will be used to illustrate some of these differences in personality as they impact spiritual formation. Some material is quite technical and hard to grasp. Don't worry about that, but do understand that the Lord works with us individually in light of His knowledge of our different personalities.

The MBTI measures preferences in four different areas. These measurements are on a continuum from one extreme to the other, with the basic recognition that every person combines some elements of each extreme.

(E) Extroversion............Introversion (I)
(S) Sensing....................Intuition (N)
(T) Thinking..................Feeling (F)
(J) Judging ....Perceiving (P)

Extroversion and Introversion: Focused Outward or Focused Inward

The first scale (Extroversion-Introversion) measures the primary focus of the individual. Some persons are primarily focused upon the outer world of persons and objects. Their psychic energy is directed toward the world outside themselves. These persons are known as *Extroverts.* They enjoy talking and laughing with others, usually in a crowd. They find renewal in relationships with many different persons. *Introverts,* on the other hand, focus their energy and interest in the internal world of ideas and being. Their range of friends is narrow, and they will reveal their inner workings only after they really get to know you.

Social skills and personal interaction are not clues to this scale. *Introverts* may be equally skillful in social interaction, but they find it tiring. While *Extroverts* find energy and renewal in interpersonal relationships, the *Introvert* finds renewal in solitude.

Immediately this preference colors spiritual development. *Extroverts* will prefer group Bible study and small-group discussion and praying together with others. If an *Extrovert* arrives at a major insight while alone, he or she can't wait to find someone with whom to share the new idea. Their interests move toward serving others and reaching out in evangelism.

Introverts will prefer private Bible study where they can quietly think through the meaning. Prayer becomes an inner experience with God that is violated if there are others around to distract. Small-group discussions leave them very uncomfortable.

In worship, the *Extrovert* will enjoy the group processes of singing and the hubbub when everyone turns around and shakes hands in order to "pass the peace." The *Introvert* prefers the quiet moments when he or she can turn inward and find spiritual renewal.

Information Gathering—by the Senses or by Intuition

The second scale (Sensing—Intuition) measures the method by which we prefer to gather information. Persons who have developed the *Sensing* skills, whether focused on the external or the internal world, have all antennae extended to pick up information. They are interested in specific and concrete realities. The here-and-now with all of its facts and details is of primary concern.

The *Intuitive,* on the other hand, use the unconscious and the imagination to focus upon possibilities in the future. They absorb information in large units without worrying about the particular. They often appear to be the dreamers with their heads in the clouds.

In categories of spiritual development the needs of these two differing approaches are quite different. In Bible study, for instance, the *Sensing* types will work with specific details in the passage under consideration. They will ask the factual questions and will use every sense to gather information. They will pray with concrete specificity—even getting lost in the details. They are very practical in approach to things spiritual—and especially to worship. The specific external features of the sanctuary will be very important to them.

The *Intuitive* types will pray with imagination and celebrate the mystery of God and His presence. They will focus upon the metaphorical and the symbolic in Bible study. In worship they will absorb the total atmosphere in their search for the divine presence.

Information Organization—by Thinking or People Values

The third scale evaluates the way persons prefer to organize the information they have gathered. The *Thinking* types use logic and analysis to organize the data they have gathered—with concern for justice, objectivity, and clarity. Frequently they are unaware of the feelings of those around them as they search for the authoritative truth that will set them free. They are often willing to sacrifice relationship for the sake of objective truth.

> **Each of us is permitted to grow in relationship with God in light of our preferences and background and distinctiveness!**

In spiritual development, the *Thinking* types are always concerned with the thought-provoking. Their favorite sermons are informative and deep. Their prayers are often written out in order to get precisely the right concept in words. Cognitive clarity in worship is a primary value. They most often become aware of God's presence after thinking a great idea. They will probably enter heaven head first.

On the other hand, the *Feeling* types organize their information (whether gathered by sensing or intuition) with concern for persons. They are more concerned with the values and relationships than with the logic of truth. They have been known to sacrifice logic in order to promote harmony among the persons involved.

Feeling types are likely to have their "hearts strangely warmed" and will probably enter heaven heart first. They will enjoy the intimacy of group prayer. They love hymns of joy and celebration that recount previous encounters with God.

These types (feeling and thinking) will behave differently depending on whether they are introverts or extroverts, perceiving or judging, sensing or intuitive.

Imagine how these differences will show up in a Bible study. Take a passage such as the story of the two disciples on the road to Emmaus beginning at Luke 24:13. The *Sensing* types will collect the facts and details in the story. Invite the *Intuitive* types to focus on the total picture and talk about the way in which the Lord responded to the seriously depressed disciples. The *Thinking* types will be ready to identify the principles involved in the interaction of Jesus with the disciples. Finally, the *Feeling* types will want to discuss the way in which different persons were affected by the events. *Extroverts* will jump into the discussion quickly and the *Introverts*, when they finally speak, will have some rich things to contribute.

Structured Versus Spontaneous

The fourth scale measures one's attitude toward life. Persons who have a strong preference on the *Judging* scale prefer order and structure with a clear plan of operations. They deal with their world in decisive and organized fashion. They are very uncomfortable with spontaneity and disorder.

Such persons will enjoy structured and liturgical services. They want devotional books that have solid answers and clear directions. They pray in the same pattern day after day and year after year. It is now more than 40 years since I shared meals regularly with my father, but I can still repeat his mealtime prayer.

The Extrovert who prefers this organized style wants a predictable *external* world. The Introvert who prefers this organized style depends upon an orderly *inner* world.

Persons who prefer *Perceiving,* on the other hand, are very uncomfortable—even bored—with predictability and standard operating procedure. They adapt to life as it happens—

always waiting for more data and other options. Spontaneity, flexibility, and serendipity are the order of the day. Again, the preference for extroversion or introversion determines how this preference appears—whether it is focused in the outer world of persons or in the inner world of ideas and being.

In spiritual disciplines, persons who prefer spontaneity will crave change. They will experiment with differing patterns of prayer. They prefer the unexpected in worship services and small-group meetings.

> **It is also a challenge to know ourselves well enough to be able to design a strategy for nurturing our relationship with God.**

It is a major challenge for a church to provide spiritual activities and guidance for these two differing personality preferences. It is also a challenge to know ourselves well enough to be able to design a strategy for nurturing our relationship with God.

Each person carries some combination of these preferences. Each of us has some preference for organization and predictability, and each of us has some preference for spontaneity and serendipity. God really has created a world of diversity and variety! How interesting this process of building a relationship with God really is!

▶ For Personal Action and Reflection ◀

So What Do You Expect Me to Do About All This?

1. Acknowledge Individuality—Your Own and Others'

Begin by acknowledging that God has created a wonderfully diverse variety of persons in His world. He seeks relationship with every type and with every combination of types. Sometimes God speaks to us through our strengths, but often

He sneaks up on us from our blind side (the function we have not carefully developed). In His matchless grace, God wants to draw us all into a dynamic spiritual development by which some day we will be whole and integrated persons who are touched by God through a wide variety of avenues.

2. Especially Cultivate Those Means of Grace That Contribute to Your Own Spiritual Development

All the means of grace are important to a maturing and growing relationship with God. Different personalities, however, will draw from the means of grace in different ways. Everyone needs Bible study, but under the guidance of the Holy Spirit, each personality type draws from that means of grace in different ways. Everyone needs corporate worship, but introverts and extroverts function differently in worship.

What a marvelous working of the Holy Spirit, that each of us is permitted to grow in relationship with God in light of our preferences and background and distinctiveness! Praise be to God!

3. Appreciate the Spirituality of Others

List some religious exercises and experiences that seem powerful to others yet leave you unmoved.

List some religious exercises that usually powerfully affect you but leave others unmoved.

Pray that God will help you relate with understanding to those who worship, publicly and privately, differently from you.

4. Scriptures for Special Study

1 Cor. 12:4-12
Eph. 4:14-16

PART **III**

Finding Companions on the Way

... within the community of believers ...

**The Lord has given us to each other
to strengthen each other's hands.**
—John Wesley
The Letters of the Rev. John Wesley, A.M.

**Help one another to carry these heavy loads,
and in this way you will fulfil the law of Christ**
(Gal. 6:2, NEB).

**May the Lord make your love mount and overflow
towards one another ... Therefore hearten one
another, fortify one another—as indeed you do**
(1 Thess. 3:12; 5:11, NEB).

Introduction to Part III
STANDING ALONE— TOGETHER

The giant redwoods of California have stood tall against the howling storms for centuries now. You would think that with such an endurance record they would have deep roots that burrow deep into the mountainside and wrap themselves around huge boulders. You could think that— but you would be wrong. Actually, they have shallow roots.

How can they survive so long? They grow in groves, and the roots of many trees entwine. Thus they stand together against the storms as if to announce to the north wind, "We stand together. If you are going to take one of us out, you will have to take us all."

Sometimes a redwood does fall, almost always one that sprouted up some distance from the others. Its roots could not reach those of the other trees. Even a giant redwood cannot stand when it has to stand alone.

Christians are like that too. We cannot stand alone; we really do need each other. The holy life is not a journey for solitary souls. The church is a called-out *community*, a group of sinners saved by grace who help each other on the way.

John Wesley was right when he organized his converts in societies, classes, bands, and in twin soul and mentoring relationships. No one can travel this road alone.

Your Redeemer knows you need companions on the way. God has called the Church to form nurturing congregations, instructional groups, intensive bands, and faith-mentoring pairs to keep His children on the highway of holiness. Our Wesleyan heritage is abundantly rich in instruction on how Christians should help each other on the road to the New Jerusalem. To this day, John Wesley's structures for Christian nurture are unsurpassed. In this section of the book we will examine this part of our heritage, looking at the modern counterparts of those marvelous means of spiritual nurture.

Far too many modern Christians try to make the spiritual life a private affair. They resist the vulnerability and accountability of community—and they thus bypass one of the required, essential dimensions of spiritual formation and holy living. If you are in that category, please open your heart to what the Spirit may teach you as you read the next several chapters about the shared Christian life.

11

The Holy Life Is a Community Affair

Meet Deborah Harrington. Life has caved in on her. Within the last three months, she has faced numerous problems. Her husband ran away with a younger woman. Her grown children said it was her fault—don't call us. She was fired from her job—"inability to concentrate." Her wallet containing her last $300 was stolen while she was in the doctor's office. The doctor told her she has diabetes. To top it all off, her electricity was shut off because of a bill she insists she paid.

Deborah is not a religious person, but now she is ready to try anything—even prayer. In her dim apartment, she falls across her unmade bed and cries out to God. She tries to remember the childhood prayers, "Now I lay me . . ." About half of the Lord's Prayer comes back to her. She weeps a while, then tries to recite other prayers. Finally, she bursts out in spontaneous tears of repentance and supplication.

Three hours go by and, as she prays, she senses a Pres-

ence, a Presence who comforts and strengthens and con-
soles—peace even in this chaos. She praises God. Hope
bubbles up, her tears stop, and she smiles.

Deborah feels she should start to church. It's Saturday
evening, so she walks the four blocks to a neighborhood
church. She knows it won't be open, but she wants to see
when the Sunday service starts. If she is going to walk
with God, she reasons, she must go to church.

The next day, Deborah, a walking cluster of heartache
and need, but also with a little flame of faith, walks into
the church. Will anyone notice? Will anyone care? She
looks at the backs of the heads of 250 worshipers as she
tries to listen to a sermon on how the church must be an
advocate for the poor and oppressed. The hour goes by.
She exits. No one took her name, spoke to her, or even
made eye contact. Deborah walks the four long blocks
home, telling herself what a fool she is. She remembers
that there is a half bottle of gin in her cupboard.

What is Deborah's spiritual life expectancy? Her tragic
story emphasizes again that both fledging believers and
veteran Christians need a nurturing community of faith.

The wisdom of 20 Christian centuries raises itself on
one elbow and in a tone that tells us we should need no reminder, informs us that none of us can long stay on the
path of the holy life if we travel alone.

One of the most dangerous popular notions is the
"myth of the individual victorious Christian life."[1] As
Reuben Welch has taught so effectively, "We really do need
each other." And that is why God in His wisdom plants
Christians in communities of faith.

Our individualistic Western culture, drunk on the
liquors of "I've Gotta Be Me" and "I Did It My Way" finds
this basic Christian truth hard to accept. But Christianity is
a community affair.

Our spiritual ancestor, John Wesley, knew this well.
He called his religious movement a "connexion." He
worked hard and successfully to keep those early Wes-

leyans "connected." He created spiritual formation structures that included societies, classes, bands, one-to-one
spiritual guidance, and a design for family religion.

If anyone among the first generation Methodists could
out-evangelize Wesley, it was his comrade in the Holy
Club and Oxford classmate, George Whitefield. But there is
more to sustaining a religious movement than mass evangelism. What do you do to nurture the converts? At this,
Wesley excelled.

Not so Whitefield—he became one of what Wesley
called "fugitive preachers" who led many people to the
Cross but quickly left the babes in Christ to starve while he
hurried on to another campaign.

In his old age, Whitefield looked back dolefully on his
career. "Brother Wesley acted wisely," he said. "The souls
that were awakened under his ministry, he joined in class,
and thus preserved the fruits of his labor. This I neglected,
and my people are a rope of sand."[2]

| **Merely getting believers together in the same building does not make a church.** |

No rope of sand for Wesley! He purposed "not to strike
one stroke in any place where I cannot follow the blow."[3] He
was convinced that even if one could preach "like an apostle," but failed to organize classes and bands, that those awakened by preaching would soon be "faster asleep than ever."[4]

Such a commitment to community is crucial in our
time when so much of what is heralded as spiritual formation is meant to be carried out in the solitude of private devotion. Steven Harper's caution is timely: "One of my
greatest apprehensions regarding spiritual formation," this
Asbury Theological Seminary professor says, "is that it will
be considered an individualized, privatized, and largely
hidden experience . . . [that] can be *practiced* alone."[5]

Let it be noted that nothing described in this book—private devotion, small-group ministry, or sacrificial service—can become a substitute for corporate worship.

A brick alone in a field is not worth much. It's something to stub your toe on. But a brick joined with other bricks in a church building helps hold up the cross, the pulpit, and the altar. Solitary Christians are as useless as solitary bricks.

. Whatever else the New Testament Church is, it is a "called-out *community* of faith." The task of the Church is fourfold: worship, evangelism, nurture, and service. The Church has nothing else to do.

The basic organization in the early Wesleyan "connexion" was the society. It functioned as a nurturing congregation. The classes and bands were subdivisions of it.

Wesley defined the *Methodist Society* as a group of persons "united in order to pray together, to receive the word of exhortation, and to watch over one another in love, that they may help each other work out their salvation."[6] This is what church membership should mean today—a mutual commitment to help each other toward God and good. Discipleship is a community affair.

CORPORATE WORSHIP IS NOT ENOUGH

The benefits of corporate worship are priceless and indispensable. Christianity simply doesn't work well except in a community of persons sharing "like precious faith." But the church has much work to do after the benediction has been pronounced and the congregation dismissed.

People like Deborah Harrington, whom you met on the first page of this chapter, need more than a song and a sermon. And so does anyone who wants to live the deeper life.

The church has to be more than an "inspiration station." Merely "getting believers together in the same building does not make a church."[7] Just looking at the backs of the heads of the worshipers sitting between you and the pulpit, or even joining hands and singing choruses together, can still leave deep hungers of the heart unfed.

The church that depends solely on large-group worship services soon becomes a "Teflon" church. A lot of people enter but don't stick. They slide right through like French toast out of a Teflon skillet. The members soon live out Whitefield's lament, becoming "a rope of sand."

Our spiritual ancestor, John Wesley, devised a system for spiritual nurture that has yet to be improved on. In fact, most successful nurturing churches use some form of Wesley's spiritual formation structures.

Wesley created a system of small-group nurture that included class meetings, band meetings, spiritual guides, select societies, a backsliders' band, and an excellent system of family religion. Figure 1 displays these structures.

> **The church that depends solely on large-group worship services soon becomes a "Teflon" church.**

The only requirement to become a member of the society was a *desire* to seek salvation in Christ. Every society member was required to be a member of a 12-person class and could volunteer to participate in a 5-person band. As needed, the use of spiritual guides, faith mentors, the select society, or the penitent band was available. In addition, family worship was a daily tradition.

Examine successful nurturing churches today, and you will see structures similar to those of John Wesley. One church I recently visited offered (besides corporate worship and Sunday School classes for all ages) Bible study groups, prayer fellowships, a divorce recovery group, a cancer support group, a preparation for membership class, and a group meeting for people leaving the homosexual life-style. In addition, special classes were being offered in leadership training, computer literacy, English as a second language, parenting, family finances, and photography.

All of these activities are good. But there is one difference. A few of the small-group functions cited in the previous paragraph have very little to do with spiritual formation and the holy life.

Figure 1

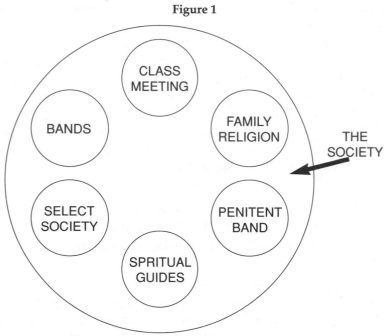

**John Wesley's Structures
for Spiritual Formation**

In the upcoming chapters we shall take a closer look at Wesley's small groups and their modern counterparts. Many modern small-group ministries deal directly with the pursuit of holiness and spiritual formation. Many others, however, reflect the consumer attitude toward ministry, which is yet another aspect of American individualism.

Some people today could not care less what the name on the church sign says, what a church believes, or what it stands for, as long as it keeps their kids off the street, strengthens their marriage, can teach them a marketable skill, makes them feel good, and makes few demands. To meet such consumer-oriented individualists at the point of their needs is wise, but that is quite different from small groups majoring in spiritual formation.

But, you say, my church doesn't offer small-group ministries. Let me refer you again to John Wesley's counsel to Frances Godfrey. "It is a blessed thing to have fellow travellers to the New Jerusalem. If you do not find them you must make them, for none can travel this road alone."[8]

▶ For Personal Action and Reflection ◀

1. What Is a Community of Faith?

A. The Church is a called-out community of faith. Scripture and 2,000 years of Christian experience have taught us that no one can live the holy life alone, that is, without the support of a faith community. That's easy enough to say, but what does *community* mean?

The word *community* is defined and described with such terms as these:

> *joint possession*
> *held in common*
> *union*
> *interdependence*
> *in communion*
> *partnership*
> *shared mutually*
> *harmony*
> *concord*
> *affinity*
> *similarity*

Antonyms or opposites of *community* include *disparity, difference, dissimilarity, disagreement, conflict,* as well as *private, personal, individual.*

B. Using the above information, write your own one-sentence definition of the Church as a community of faith.

---

2. What Is a Nurturing Congregation?

A. The focus of chap. 11 has to do with how a "nurturing congregation" helps Christians find and live the holy life. Read the introduction to Part III and chap. 11 carefully. *Nurture* comes from the same Latin word from which we get the term *nurse.* It is defined and described with these terms: *nourish, feed, sustain, strengthen, tutor, educate, instruct, develop, shape, guide, discipline,* and *encourage.* Its antonyms include *neglect, ignore, overlook,* and *deprive.*

B. Christian nurture is also one of the themes in Galatians. Browse through this Epistle again, marking words and phrases that refer to nurture. Study Gal. 4:19 and all of chapter 5.

   1. What is the aim of "spiritual formation" according to Gal. 4:19?

   2. Which avenue is most likely to lead to the formation of Christ within: devoted legalism or freedom in Christ? (See Galatians 5.)

   3. What are the limits of the Christian's freedom? Is the believer free to do whatever he or she wishes? (See Gal. 5:13.)

   4. Consider the works of the flesh and the "harvest" they produce (Gal. 5:19-21). The "harvest" or "fruit" of the Spirit are quite different (v. 22). In fact, they are the opposites of the works of the flesh. For example, *peace* or *stillness of heart,* as the word is best translated, is the opposite of *strife, anger,* and *envy.* Make further comparisons in your own study of the passage.

3. Is My Church a Nurturing Congregation?

A. List the ministries (formal and informal) at your church that aim at Christian nurture.

B. In what ways have you helped your church become a nurturing church? What would you be willing to do to make the community of faith that is your church even more effective in its nurturing ministry?

What part of the church program provides an arena for people to talk to each other about the things that burden them most?

12

Face to Face
and Heart to Heart

He sat there quietly in his socially acceptable dark suit with tears streaming down his face. Our hour and one-half for the workshop on small-group ministries had sped by. The small-group workshop was a sort of sidebar in a District Sunday School Convention. I introduced a few basic concepts about small-group ministries, including a few comments about our indebtedness to Wesley's class meeting. Then I engaged the 12 people, who had chosen this seminar over seven others being offered at the same time, in a demonstration exercise.

We worked for nearly an hour with the "Four Quaker Questions": (1) *Where did you live between the ages of 7 and 12?* (2) *How did you heat your home then?* (3) *What or who was the center of human warmth in your family?* (4) *When, if ever, did God become more than a mere word to you?* At the end of this session the gentleman in the dark suit was in tears.

As unthreateningly as I could, I asked why he was weeping. He wiped his eyes with a red silk handkerchief and said, "I've served on the board of my church for 35 years. Everyone in this room was a stranger to me an hour ago. But I know them right now better than I know the people I have worked and worshiped with for 35 years."

The sad fact is that we can go to church every Sunday and never really get to know anyone. We worship with others, notice the backs of their heads during the choir anthem and the sermon, shake hands and greet them with a pasted-on smile after the service—and never get within a heartbeat of them. The members of some churches are no more likely to get to know each other than are spectators at a football game. Not really knowing each other, they are unable to help each other "grow strong in the broken places."

This did not happen in John Wesley's structures for mutual pastoral care. As mentioned earlier, every member of the society was required to join a class of about 12 persons, which met every week. The agenda of the meeting included instruction, encouragement, dialogue, and strict accountability.

Many believe the class meeting was Wesley's greatest contribution to Christianity. D. L. Moody declared that it was the best instrument for training converts that the world has ever seen. Henry Ward Beecher affirmed that it was Wesley's greatest gift to the world. John Drakeford wrote that the openness of the class meeting where pretense was stripped away provided the individuals with "an experience they would never get in a church today."[1]

We desperately need something like the class meeting in our churches today. Some believe the adult Sunday School class has successfully replaced the class meeting. Make no mistake: adult Sunday School classes make a great contribution as part of a nurturing church. But what they do best is quite different from what our spiritual ancestors derived from the class meeting. The level of personal sharing in an open meeting like a large Sunday School class is far lower than what occurred in the Wesleyan class meeting. The accountability level is also weaker. In the class meeting, the leader questioned each person about his or her spiritual progress, temptations, trials, failures, and victories.

In one large church in the Midwest, I set out to organize spiritual life fellowship groups in the adult Sunday School classes. I arranged to have veteran Christians and new Christians in each group, along with a prospect or two, so that the whole range of the church's work would be put before the spiritual gifts of the group members. I had hardly gotten started when a group of young adults in the 35- to 40-year-old bracket came to me and asked if I would help them form a group and lead it. I did not want to do it, but I couldn't turn them down either.

> **Face-to-face groups fostering acceptance, belonging, instruction, and accountability are not peripheral spiritual serendipities but are at the heart of the church's mission.**

I knew the entire group. They were well-to-do professionals. I watched them week after week drive into the parking lot in their Cadillacs, swish down the aisles in their fur coats with their perfect families. The 12 persons in the group had 21 college degrees.

As I drove across town en route to our first meeting at an attorney's home, I prayed about the group and about my reluctant attitude to take the time to work with a group of solid, perfect Christians who had no real needs. I prayed that the Lord would help us not waste each other's time.

We sat in the lawyer's parlor, and I started out with a low-key, nonthreatening exercise. Respond to this question, I said: "When was the last time you cried?"

I was not prepared for the answers. It took us three and one-half hours to answer this starter question. Every one of those successful, highly educated persons had been in tears within the previous two weeks, men and women alike. I could not believe it. I had watched them come to church in their Sunday best, I had served on boards and committees with them, and I had not one clue that each one of them was a walking cluster of heartache and need. The group I had reluctantly started met regularly for three years—and how we needed each other during those times. Each one of us affirmed more than once, to use John Wesley's words, "The Lord . . . has given us to each other, that we may strengthen each other's hands."[2]

Each of these persons was a member of the most dynamic Sunday School class in that local church. It had a pair of gifted teachers and a full round of social activities. Yet these people had no arena in which to talk about the things that burdened them most.

How Important Can Face-to-face Groups Be?

"I'm sure meeting with other Christians for instruction, sharing, and prayer would be good," she told me, "but I'm way overcommitted already. I've got PTA, Little League, bowling, choir practice, and I sell Avon besides working my regular job."

> **If our church calendars must be shoved around in order to make room for face-to-face meetings, then let the shoving begin.**

Though I couldn't find many things on her list that outranked Christian nurture through face-to-face groups, I took no for an answer and got out of her way.

Our spiritual ancestors who peopled those historic Wesleyan class meetings had quite another priority list. Those pious folks would undergo great harassment, walk great distances, and endure all sorts of persecution and hardship in order to "meet the class." Those early classes functioned in much the same mode as the house churches of the Early Church, which was itself a small-group movement.

The early Methodist class and society meetings attracted persecution and violence from the reckless mobs, often inspired by Anglican clergy and conveniently ignored by law enforcement officials. Meetings were broken up, class members assaulted, and homes of Methodists burned down. Note this report from the *Cambridge Journal and Weekly Flying Post* for May 18, 1745.

Exeter: Monday evening, May 6, as the Methodists assembled together in a house . . . behind the Guildhall, a large Mob was gathered at the Door, who pelted them as they went in, and daubed them with Dung, Potatoes, Mud, etc., and before they came out were increased to some thousands, . . . who, as the people came out threw them in the Dirt, trampled on them, and beat all without Exception, so that many fled from them without their hats and wigs, . . . coats, or with half of them tore off; and the women they used most inhumanly, some they lamed, others stripp'd almost naked, and rol'd in the most indecent manner in the Kennel [ditch], besmearing their faces with Lampblack, flour and mud; thus they continued till near Twelve at Night, when they thought fit to disperse.

What real needs such society and class meetings must have met! How valuable they must have been for our spiritual ancestors to put themselves to such risk in order to attend these meetings!

FELLOWSHIP AND ACCOUNTABILITY

The class meeting provided an arena for Christian koinonia. Acceptance, love, and commitment to each other were the keynotes. One purpose of the class, John Wesley said, was "to inspect their outward walking, to inquire of their inward state; to learn what are their trials; and how they fall by or conquer them."[3] This "inspection" was not that of a religious bully policeman but the pastoral work of a caring class leader.

A typical meeting would start with hymn singing. Then the class leader would share the condition of her or his own spiritual life. Answers to prayer, temptations, grief, failures, and spiritual progress were reported in extemporaneous testimony. Following the leader's example, others would share their needs and blessings. In this manner the leader soon learned "whether they now . . . enjoy the life of God. Whether they grow therein or decay; if they decay what is the cause; and what the cure."[4] Since some of the sharing was quite personal, visitors were allowed to attend only every other (alternate) meetings.

Instruction was often included in the class meeting, often in response to a practical question or to something that had been preached in the society meeting. Part of the aim of the classes was to "instruct the ignorant in the principles of religion; if need be to repeat, to explain, or enforce what has been said in the public preaching."[5]

At *every* small-group meeting an offering was taken for the poor.

Full consecration of the believer was earnestly taught. Wesley coached his leaders to lead their flock to "being wholly devoted to God," to "conquer self-will" in "all its disguises," make "Christ their all," and "oppose self-love in all its hidden forms."[6] Spiritual growth and Christian perfection were the constant targets of the class. Wesley instructed his leaders to instill a clear conviction "that without inward . . . holiness no man shall see the Lord" and that "having received the Lord Jesus Christ, will profit us nothing unless we steadily walk in him."[7] Without the class meeting, few of those early Wesleyans would have found that deeper life for which they are so well known.

The class leader was the key to the success of the Methodist movement. He was "to visit each person in his class . . . to inquire how their souls prosper; to advise, reprove, comfort, or exhort as occasion may require; and to receive what they were willing to give to the poor."[8] Sounds a lot like Gal. 6:1-5, doesn't it?

ACCOUNTABILITY AND SERVICE

To be a member of the society you had to be active in a class. And you could not function as a member of a class without a quarterly ticket. Every class was visited every quarter by one of the traveling preachers. Every member was interviewed personally. If the interviewee had a good testimony and had missed no more than 3 of the previous quarter's 13 meetings, he was issued a new ticket—a card with his name, a slogan or verse of scripture, and a date on it. If he did not qualify, he could no longer be a card-carrying Methodist.

It is hard for us to imagine how important that card was. Remember: these people lived in a brutal society that treated the poor worse than dirt, only 1 child in 25 went to any kind of school at all, and 90% of the population lived in poverty. To these nameless nobodies, the privilege of being card-carrying Methodists was not taken lightly. It meant that they were important, that they belonged, and that someone cared for them.

Another kind of accountability, not unrelated to spiritual formation, flourished in the classes and bands. At *every* class and band meeting, without exception, these poor people gave an offering for the poor. Many times these devout people gave what they desperately needed themselves to relieve the starvation of others.

FACE-TO-FACE GROUPS IN YOUR CHURCH

It would be a mistake to woodenly re-create every detail of the Methodist class meeting. But the class meeting does remind us that Christians today need more than worship services and Sunday School classes. Face-to-face groups that provide instruction, acceptance, belonging, positive accountability, open dialogue, and spiritual guidance are not peripheral spiritual serendipities but are at the heart of the church's mission. If our church calendars must be shoved around in order to make room for face-to-face meetings, then let the shoving begin.

The very least a church can do is to organize adult Sunday School classes for pastoral care that include face-to-face groups designed to meet the current needs of class members.

▶ For Personal Action and Reflection ◀

1. Face-to-face Groups at Your Church

A. If you were to help your church put face-to-face groups aimed at spiritual formation and holy living at the heart of the church's ministry, to whom would you talk first? What planning would have to be done? Would a few pilot groups be worthwhile? What printed resources would you need?

B. Guidelines for Groups

As you plan face-to-face groups, keep these guidelines in mind.

Every group needs

(1) to make participation voluntary. Groups made of draftees *never* work.

(2) a stated and agreed-upon purpose.

(3) a capable and committed leader who is spiritually and psychologically healthy and who has a pastoral spirit.

(4) a set of mutually agreed-upon disciplines or ground rules. Typical group disciplines include

   a. Faithful attendance at every meeting

   b. A pledge to speak of nothing to others that happens in the group except what God has done for you

   c. Prayer for each member of the group by name every day

   d. Full participation in the other programs of the local church

   e. Agreement not to invite visitors to the group without approval of the whole group

2. Bible Study and Devotion

A. Use Gal. 6:1-5 in a spiritual reading exercise.

B. Read carefully the words of "In Christ There Is No East or West" (Hymn 678 in *Sing to the Lord*).

C. Record in your journal insights and inspirations, ideas, names, and faces that come to you as you study the Bible lesson and the hymn.

**One group of ten persons, learning truly to love
one another, experiencing an ever-deepening
commitment to Christ, . . . will exert more
redemptive influence in a community than a
church of one thousand uncommitted members.**

—G. Byron Deshler
The Power of the Personal Group

13

Without Reserve
and Without Disguise

Newsbreak: another drug-related murder. This time two
people were killed over a pickup truck load of marijuana.
So what else is new? I thought as I drove across town on a
springtime afternoon. But what the reporter said next
pierced me as though I had been stabbed with an icicle. A
young man had been arrested and charged with the
killings. The radio spat out his name—a name I recognized. The son of a couple in my Christian Life Fellowship
Group had been jailed, accused of murder!

That evening my wife and I went to their house. We
didn't call; we just showed up. After all, we were members of
the same small group. We got there about 7:30 P.M.—and we
were the last ones to arrive. The other members of our group
had done just what we did. One couple was out of town and
they phoned in their pledge of prayer and support. The six
other people in the group just showed up unannounced. We
didn't know what to say or do. But with one of our couples in

the biggest trouble of their lives, we just wanted to be with them, even if all we could do was share hugs and tears.

The pastor of our church had not yet gotten the news. He was away at an official meeting of some sort. But the small group members had, and they canceled whatever was on their agendas and just showed up on the doorstep of their hurting friends.

Wouldn't it be great if every Christian had a group of soul friends who would be there for them when life deals them a hammer blow?

Another couple in that same group had a 14-year-old daughter who took up with a bearded drug addict twice her age. Debbie turned up pregnant. Then she ran off with her addict boyfriend to nobody knew where. One Sunday morning her father, a lay leader in our church, was on the platform to make an announcement in the morning worship service. He was called off the platform. He handed his notes to a staff minister and left.

None of us could find our friend, Rick, or his wife, Doris, after the service. Someone said he had left the platform to answer a long-distance call. We all wondered. We all prayed, and we hoped it was news (could it be good news?) about Debbie. Two couples drove by their house to find out for sure, and the other three couples phoned.

Wouldn't it be great if every parent who gets taught how badly you can be hurt by a wayward child had 10 people to hold onto as Rick and Doris did?

"I probably will never see you again," Sheila said. It was Homecoming Sunday, and I had gone back to participate as a former pastor. I was taken aback by Sheila's remark. Trying to be cheerful, I said, "Never see me again—what are you doing, moving to Hawaii or something?"

"No," she said. "They tell me I will never get well—six months at the most."

My heart sank. I knew that during the previous year Sheila's only brother and her father had died. She read my face.

"Don't feel sorry for me. I'm OK. I'm stronger than I've ever been. And do you know why? You put me in a small group—and there I found myself as a person and as a Christian. I could never have made it without that group."

Wouldn't it be great if, when we get the worst news of all, there was a band of people who would usher us into God's presence on the cushion of their love and prayers? People who loved us so much they would do anything for us, people we could trust and talk to without reserve and without disguise, even in the solemn day of death?

FRIENDS IN COVENANT GROUPS

This is exactly the kind of care that those early Wesleyans found in their bands. Wesley felt that it was in the bands that the Wesleyan movement most precisely practiced the religion of the Early Church. He also believed that Methodism did its best spiritual formation work in the bands.

> **Have you disappointed yourself lately, spiritually speaking? How can we be most helpful in restoring you?**

Besides being a member of the society and a class, any Methodist serious about pursuing Christian perfection could become a member of a band. The band was a group of four to six persons who met weekly to share their spiritual journeys in a very intimate fellowship. These persons were bound to each other by solemn pledges of love and support. They engaged in "close conversation." They desired, Wesley said, "closer union" and wanted a group before which they could "pour out their hearts without reserve, particularly with regard to the sin which did still beset them and the temptations which were most apt to prevail over them."[1]

The bands were not for everyone. Membership was voluntary, and typically some 20 to 30 percent of society members at any one time were also band members. This meant that the bands were made up of the most devout and the most mature Christians in the society.

The results were remarkable. Wesley said that he noted that one particular person had "learned more from one hour's close disclosure [in a band] than in ten years of [listening to] public preaching."[2] Wesley believed that the success of the movement hinged on strong functioning bands.

The bands were organized by group commonality. That is, they were arranged according to sex, age, marital status, etc. The class was highly leader-oriented, but the bands were much more democratic, the leader being little more than a convener. The several members took the initiative to share their progress or lack thereof. Unusually strong bonds of love, loyalty, and mutual accountability were forged in these utterly frank and honest encounters among "companions on the way to the New Jerusalem." No visitors were allowed, and membership was always preceded by a "trial" period. The goal ever before them was spiritual formation and Christian perfection.

Wesley drew up five "starter questions" to be used in every band meeting.

1. What known sins have you committed since our last meeting?

2. What temptations have you met with?

3. How were you delivered?

4. What have you thought, said, or done, of which you doubt whether it be sin or not?

5. Have you nothing you desire to keep secret?[3]

MODERN CONTERPARTS OF THE "WITHOUT RESERVE AND WITHOUT DISGUISE" GROUPS

To many reserved Englishmen, the rules and questions seemed an outrageous invasion of privacy. Some writers renounced the bands as improper, unhealthy, and scandalous. In particular, they found them too personal and too much like the Roman Catholic confessional.

It remained for 20th-century Christians to rediscover this valuable tool for spiritual formation. "In the fellowship of such a group," wrote G. Byron Deshler, "personal problems are raised, sin and failure confessed, aspirations shared, prayer requested, and victories attested. This was the fellowship of the Early Church, and it is the kind of fellowship that must be reintroduced into the Church today if its vitality and redemptive power are to be restored."[4]

Deshler goes on to state the Church's rediscovery of bandlike small groups with these words. "One group of ten persons, learning truly to love one another, experiencing an ever-deepening commitment to Christ, . . . will exert more redemptive influence in a community than a church of one thousand uncommitted members."[5] What our spiritual forbears discovered in the band meetings needs to be rediscovered today. Millions of contemporary Christians have no small group of covenanted friends to whom they can pour out their hearts "without reserve and without disguise."

> **I trust there shall never be lacking a little company of you to watch over one another in love.**

Wesley's rules and starter questions for the bands were not weapons for some spiritual Gestapo. Rather, they were guidelines for Christians who desired to watch over each other in love. The starter questions were not designed for parlor games or get-acquainted exercises. They were for dear friends soberly seeking to help each other live holy lives.

The starter questions seem stark, blunt, harsh, and negative to us. But when you probe their intent, one finds pastoral care, not police brutality. Their positive underlying principles appear when we restate them in words compatible with our own personal, social, and spiritual sensibilities. I have restated the band questions and used them with groups in small-town churches and big-city churches, with laypersons, with seminary students, and with ministerial groups. In every setting, these restated starter questions for bandlike groups seem to be singularly blessed by the Lord.

Here is how those five starter questions sound in a contemporary group.

1. Instead of, "What sins have you committed since our last meeting?" ask, "Have you had any spiritual failures recently? Have you been disappointed with yourself lately, spiritually speaking? How can we be most helpful in restoring or supporting you? When we pray for and with you today, at what point should we focus our prayers?"

2. Instead of, "What temptations have you met with?" ask, "What temptations or spiritual problems have you been battling lately? At what points in your life do you feel most vulnerable? most weak right now? most under pressure?"

3. Instead of "How were you delivered?" ask, "If you have been delivered from any temptations lately, would you share with us how the victory was won? Would you share with us how you found the strength to endure?"

4. Instead of, "What have you thought, said, or done, of which you doubt whether it be sin or not?" ask, "Has the Lord revealed anything to you about your heart and life that makes you want to take a prayerful second look at your attitudes, life-style, service, or motivations?"

5. Instead of "Have you nothing you desire to keep secret?" ask, "Is there a spiritual problem so deep or so personal that you have never been able to talk to anyone about it? Can you even talk with God about it? Are you carrying excess baggage from the past that still today keeps you defeated and depressed? Would you like to share it with us, your spiritual partners?

Or, at least, let us pray for you about it—would you set a time each day (or this week) when you are going to pray about this matter so we can at the very same time pray for you wherever we are?"

THE PENITENT BANDS

I wish there was a way to revive one of Wesley's special groups—the penitent band. John Wesley was very realistic about backsliders. The "backsliders' band" was especially designed for sincere people who, for some reason, kept being recaptured by some besetting sin. They wanted to do right but had not yet found the discipline and strength to completely forsake their sins and stay on the path to perfection. Wesley saw that "they wanted advice and instructions suited to their case; . . . I separated them from the rest and desired them to meet me apart on Saturday evenings."[6] The format of the meetings and the techniques used are unknown at this time, but they apparently operated for many years with success.

What if all pilgrims in our churches could turn to penitent bands for support when they found themselves slipping spiritually? How many spiritual failures could be prevented if it were possible to go to a "backsliders' band" without losing face or respect? Why should it be disgraceful to admit spiritual problems and seek help? What would happen to the spiritual temperature of our churches if we could reestablish this part of our Wesleyan heritage in every local church?

COVENANT BANDS WORK TODAY

The band meeting heritage still bears fruit today. I think of Myrna. She was one of those you could count on to "come forward" each year at the annual revival. She would pray her way to faith—again, but after a few months, like one suffering from a slow bleeding of the soul, her faith would seep away.

She believed the Bible and loved the church, but full

and free salvation—especially for her—was more than her faith could bear. "It's just too good to be true," she would sometimes say.

Nothing seemed to help. Then I engaged her in a band-like small group that met on Tuesday mornings. One morning she opened her heart to the new friends she had learned to trust. Out poured her story. It was a nightmare of low self-esteem. She was born an illegitimate child. She never knew who her father was. Her mother regarded Myrna as the "biggest mistake of her life" and as the roadblock to her career.

> ## She was making sure that these little urchins knew that *somebody* cared for them.

When Myrna's mom married, the little girl was 6 years old—and excess baggage that her mother was forced to drag into her new marriage. Myrna's stepfather was alternately kind and cruel to her. To him, she was a walking reminder of his wife's former promiscuity. This idea was not unrelated to the sexual abuse she had to endure from her stepfather that began when she was 10. When she tearfully told her mother about the abuse, her mother thrashed her with a belt that left welts for weeks and promised her more of the same if she ever brought up the subject again.

When Myrna left home as a teenager, she married the only kind of man who would (in her mind) want a piece of dirt like her—a drunken alcoholic.

Poor Myrna: she thought that not even God could love her—that is, until her group members poured out acres of love and acceptance. Slowly, Myrna came to realize that these people knew all about her—and loved her all the more. Maybe, after all, Jesus really did die for her too.

To make a long story short, Myrna was soon involved in teacher training. We gave her a class of four young children. After about three months, I visited her classroom. The four had grown to nine. An increase of five in three months—that's nothing special. Maybe not. But I wish you could have seen them. Myrna's new pupils did not have nice Sunday clothes, or shiny new shoes. In fact, Myrna had gone out and rounded up five of the most neglected little urchins in our town. She who once thought she was unloved and unwanted was making sure that these neglected little ones knew that *somebody* really did care about them.

I wish for every Christian in the world what John Wesley hoped for Ellen Gretton and her band. "I trust there shall never be wanting [lacking] a little company of you to watch over one another in love."[7]

▶ For Personal Action and Reflection ◀

1. People Stories

This chapter contains four anecdotes about people whose lives were turned around by the loving care of a small covenant group (Myrna, Sheila, Rick, Doris, and the family cited on the opening page of this chapter).

Can you name some people you know who have been "rescued" by a Christian small group? If you cannot think of any such person, to what do you attribute that startling fact?

2. An Important Question

Do you have a group of covenanted friends with whom you can speak "without reserve and without disguise"?

If your answer is no, what can you do to change that?

3. Bible Study

Read 1 Thess. 4:1-8. In this passage Paul advises his friends about:

A. Immorality, uncleanness, passion, and lust

B. Sanctification, holiness, honor, pleasing God, and obeying the Holy Spirit

Considering the negative list *(a)* and the positive list *(b),* do you think that a person who meets every week with a group of persons who pray for him or her every day, show interest in his or her spiritual progress, and holds him or her in gentle accountability is more likely to stay on the straight and narrow than a Christian who tries to go it alone?

4. Flying High

Wild geese fly in Vs because, by flying in formation, they can fly nearly twice as far as they can alone. You see, the updraft created by the wings of a goose makes it easier for the next bird in line to fly.

In what ways are Christians like that? Could you make "flying" a little easier for someone this week?

Such was our affection for you that we chose rather to
share with you not only the gospel of God but our very
selves, so dear had you become to us
(1 Thess. 2:8).[1]

14

Wing to Wing and Oar to Oar: Spiritual Friends and Faith Mentors

We sat on a bench under a giant eucalyptus tree enjoying one of those glorious June afternoons in Marin County, California. My new friend and I spoke of things theological, philosophical, and political. He looked at his watch. "Oh, I've got to get going," he said. "I've got a mentoring meeting in less than an hour."

"A what?" I asked.

"A mentoring meeting. You see, our church has this mentoring program. About 30 professional men and women in our church make themselves available to high school juniors and seniors. If a teen is interested in law, medicine, dentistry, teaching, or banking—whatever—they can sign up with one of us."

"Sign up?" I asked.

"Yes, for a year we mentor the youngster in our profession. He or she accompanies us through our work—getting an inside look at law, medicine, or professoring (that's me)," he replied.

"Is it strictly business?" I queried.

"Oh, no. We spend social time together as well. And the kids usually have some real basic questions about the Christian faith too."

"You feel like it's a good investment, I take it," I said.

"Let's put it this way. At least 25 young people from our church have gone into the profession of their local church mentor. That's 25 Christian professionals that our church has put on the map, so to speak."

Kind of dumbstruck, I muttered, "How utterly Wesleyan."

"No," he replied, "we are all Presbyterians."

> **Their shared tombstone reads,**
> **"Wing to wing, and oar to oar."**

He was right, of course, but I was right, too, because those early Wesleyans practiced one-to-one faith mentoring. In addition to societies, classes, and bands, John Wesley modeled and taught one-to-one spiritual guidance.

I did not know this until I spent one whole summer studying nearly 3,000 of Wesley's letters. I catalogued and indexed them according to some 125 spiritual formation categories. What I discovered was hundreds of letters in which Wesley referred one believer to another Christian for counsel and advice.

The classes and bands have hogged center stage in the Wesley scholar's inquiries, but it appears that from Mr. Wesley down to every lay preacher in the movement, a regular practice of one-to-one spiritual guidance was carried on. Two sorts of spiritual guidance were commonly practiced. Frequently, Wesley brought together a "babe in

Christ" (new convert) and a veteran Christian, often called a "spiritual father" or a "nursing mother." Even more frequently, Wesley brought together "twin souls." These were persons who had much in common personally and spiritually. Often these matches resulted in lifelong friendships and long years of mutual spiritual guidance.

Wesleyan spiritual guidance was not the sort that could be called "spiritual direction." Spiritual *direction* too often requires the person to completely submit to the will of the director. That dangerous practice produces too many "hounds who devour the hare," to use Tauler's metaphor. The keynotes to Wesleyan faith mentoring were and are *voluntariness* and *mutuality*.

WHO NEEDS A FAITH MENTOR OR A SPIRITUAL FRIEND?

Don't skip this section. The answer, whether you are a veteran Christian or a fledgling, may be *you!*

Faith Mentors

Who needs a faith mentor more than new converts, weak Christians, or sincere Christians who have repeatedly tried to live the holy life—only to fail again and again?

Such persons to be sure need a faith mentor, a "spiritual father" or "nursing mother," as Wesley called such fosterers of faith. A faith mentor is one who travels with us on our faith journey, pointing the way, teaching us life and spiritual skills, modeling the holy life, holding us accountable, providing a caring and trustworthy environment, and helping us discern God's will for our own spiritual vocation or calling.

A faith mentor or spiritual father serves as "God's usher." He or she practices the "art of arts." A faith mentor should be characterized by love, tender respect, holiness detachment, and theological competence. He or she should possess the gift of discernment, much patience, practice utter frankness and honesty, and be available to God the Holy Spirit.[2]

Such persons John Wesley habitually assigned to offer pastoral care to new or weak converts. Wesley often referred to his practice as putting "babes in Christ under the care of 'spiritual fathers.'"

Contemporary writer Kenneth Leech says a good faith mentor or spiritual guide should have the following qualities.

1. A person possessed by the Spirit
2. A person characterized by holiness of life and closeness to God
3. A person of experience—in prayer and life
4. A person of learning—particularly in the Scriptures
5. A person of discernment who can read the signs of the times and the writing on the wall of the soul
6. A person who gives way to the Holy Spirit.[3]

Could you use the personal help of a person like that?

JOHN WESLEY AS SPIRITUAL MENTOR

Wesley was convinced that spiritual guidance was essential for all. He repeatedly warned his people that they could not keep warm alone. To Mary Bosanquet he wrote, "You have need of a steady guide, and one that knows you well."[4] His letter to Ann Bolton, July 8, 1785, shows Wesley's idea of both the necessity of a spiritual guide and the qualities he expected in a good spiritual guide: "My Dear Nancy,—It is undoubtedly expedient for you to have a friend in whom you can fully confide that may be always near you or at a small distance, and ready to be consulted on all occasions . . . I am glad, therefore, that a good Providence has given you one . . . You may certainly trust her in every instance; and she has both understanding, piety, and experience."[5]

John Wesley modeled, as well as taught, faith mentoring. If you want to see exactly how faith mentoring works, study the letters of John Wesley to Ann Bolton. He wrote some 130 letters of spiritual guidance to her over 29 years. When Ann was a teenager, John (40 years her senior) influenced her not to go through with her planned marriage to an unbeliever. Thereafter, John Wesley felt a sense of responsibility for her welfare. As a young adult, Ann had a feeble faith; nevertheless, it was growing under Wesley's guidance. She fervently sought sanctifying grace or Christian perfection for several years. She wrote to Wesley, saying that for all her seeking she feared that she was "far away from holiness." Her mentor replied, "How far are you from holiness? Nay, rather think how near you are to it! You are not farther from it than you are from faith, than you are from Christ. And how far is He from you? Is He not nigh? Is He not just now knocking at the door of your heart? Hark! The Master calleth you!"[6]

> **I am fully persuaded that if you had always one or two faithful friends near you who would speak the very truth from their heart and watch over you in love, you would swiftly advance.**

Eventually, Wesley was able to write to Ann in celebration, "It gives me very much pleasure to hear . . . that God . . . has established your soul in pure love and given you the abiding witness of it." In the same letter, he refers Ann to two other women (Hannah Bell and Patty Chapman), who "have the same deep experience." Ann was to converse with them that "each might be profited by the other."[7]

But the holy life does not end with a glorious entrance into it. Suffering in the form of grief for the death of all her family, and a disabling illness challenged Ann. Her faith mentor was there for her during those years. Wesley wrote her many letters of consolation and encouragement. "He that made the Captain of your salvation perfect through sufferings has called you to walk in the same path."[8] Again he wrote, "I feel much sympathy with you in your troubles which endear you to me exceedingly."[9] When he was 85 years old, Wesley wrote Ann (then 45), "I love you the more because you are a daughter of affliction."[10]

As a faith mentor, Wesley led Ann Bolton into sanctifying grace, through the hazards of sorrow and suffering—and beyond sanctification and suffering to outstanding Christian service. Wesley came to call her the "nursing mother" of all the classes, bands, and prayer meetings around Witney. Wesley referred many troubled women to her for mentoring. Wesley told those whom he referred to Ann that she was a "perfect pattern of true womanhood."[11]

Frequently, persons who can offer the spiritual fathering type of mentoring are mature people who know life and the Christian's walk. Persons who need them are often young or new Christians, or those who are weak in the faith.

> **A faith mentor must have the ability to understand without judging, . . . the ability to be with another in pain.**

Many of our older Christians, however, are either too busy trying to act like the young people or are too willing to turn everything over to the "younger folk" and just coast into old age. Carl Jung reminds us, "We cannot live the afternoon of life according to the program of life's morning. The afternoon must have a significance of its own and cannot be merely a pitiful appendage."[12] The most significant question facing our mature Christians is the choice of *stagnation* or *generativity*. Sharon Parks speaks this prophetic word, "The generativity of the adult is dependent upon meaningful, faithful connection with the next generation. To accompany the young adult in faith can mean a reawakening of one's own potential for compassion, excellence, and vocation."[13]

But let's go back to our question, Who needs a faith mentor?

I have developed a Spiritual Formation Inventory questionnaire. Individuals or groups cite their perceived spiritual strengths and weaknesses by marking the questionnaire. The document probes 21 areas vital to living the deeper Christian life.

I have administered the survey to several different groups, including seminary students, pastors, laity classes, and retreat participants. Further, under my supervision, pastors of about a dozen evangelical churches have used the instrument to establish a spiritual formation "profile" of their congregations.

One question consistently receives the lowest marks. Here it is—question seven:

> How would you rate your success in finding a faith mentor or soul friend with whom you can share "anything" about your spiritual life?

5	4	3	2	1
Very Satisfied	Satisfied	Sometimes Satisfied	Seldom Satisfied	Not at All Satisfied

The groups with which I have worked came up with a score of about 1.6. Who needs a faith mentor or spiritual friend? Just about all of us. In group after group, people are telling me, "We don't have anyone to talk to."

Poet Robert Frost and his wife lie buried side by side in a New England cemetery. The inscription on their shared tombstone reads: "Wing to wing, and oar to oar." Christians are telling me that when it comes to their spiritual journey, they have no one with whom to travel "Wing to wing, and oar to oar."

Spiritual Friends

"Go off and don't eat until you get a soul friend, because anyone without a soul friend is like a body without a head."[14] So said the Irish St. Brigid in the *Book of Leinster*. The ancient Celtic Irish had a name for soul friend—*anam-*

chara. When they used that word, everyone knew what they meant.

The type of mentoring called by the labels *soul friend* or *spiritual friend* is the type of spiritual guidance that goes on between spiritual peers. In this mentoring arrangement, no *senior* or *junior* status is obvious. Rather, it is a case of "twin souls" mentoring each other.

John Wesley believed that even the strongest Christians needed spiritual friends in order to live the holy life. To the exemplary banker, Ebenezer Blackwell, he wrote, "I am fully persuaded that if you had always one or two faithful friends near you who would speak the very truth from their heart and watch over you in love, you would swiftly advance."[15]

WHAT DOES A FAITH MENTOR LOOK LIKE?

Persons interested in finding or becoming faith mentors can profit from reviewing the qualities God uses in such persons.

1. A faith mentor is sensitive about relationships. Sondra Matthaei says that "faith mentors are persons in relationship with God and with other persons as co-creators."[16] That is to say that a person who is a devout Christian and a friendly person can make an effective faith mentor. Through relationships, the faith mentor participates in divinely ordained transformation. Robert Evans says, "Transformation is the transpersonal embodiment of God's grace."[17]

2. A faith mentor embodies the grace of God. "A faith mentor or spiritual friend is a living representative of God's grace, a person who has experienced God's grace . . . and through grace-full living extends that grace to others."[18] That is to say that a faith mentor incarnates (however imperfectly) the gospel of Jesus Christ. Tilden Edwards said that "our physical form is an ambiguous embodiment of the Spirit."[19]

3. A faith mentor knows how to listen with acceptance and

respect. A faith mentor has the gift and "the ability to understand without judging, the ability to hear what another is attempting to put into words, the ability to be with another in pain."[20]

An accepting environment is utterly essential to any faith mentoring or soul friend relationship. A person who indulges in quick legalistic judgmentalism is not the person to turn a tender soul over to. Effective soul friends can hear the worst about you and still love and care for you and help you toward God's redeeming grace and His liberating will. Such a faith mentor reflects something akin to the unconditional love of our Lord.

The effective faith mentor listens to your story with respect for you, your experiences, your joys, and sorrows. He or she will not brush your story aside in order to tell his or her "more important" story.

Self-disclosure to a spiritual friend can be redemptive. It may become more than an encounter with a godly person. It may be an encounter with my deeper self, an encounter which, as Augustine recorded in his *Confession,* forces me "to look in my own face."[21]

4. *A faith mentor can often discern the moving of God's Spirit.* "Discernment is the awareness of God at work in our own lives and in the lives of others."[22] Strangely enough, faith mentors may discern God at work in our confusions, failures, problems, and successes before we ourselves do. They discern His will and presence and help us make meaning of life's shambles.

Tim reported how a mentor helped him make meaning in a time of tragedy. "He got me in touch with grief as an expression or source of grace that I didn't know existed. He opened up a whole new realm in which I could know God."[23]

The mentor's gift of discernment may go so far as to help us imagine or foresee the meaningful future God has for us, a future that we could not imagine without help. I have heard and read a number of testimonies of persons who entered a fruitful vocation of ministry because a mentor "saw" them in ministry before they themselves ever imagined a career in ministry.

5. *A faith mentor has the quality of vulnerable openness in relationships.* A true spiritual friend not only permits you to speak openly of your own problems, failures, and joys but also practices appropriate self-disclosure and vulnerability. Often, a spiritual friend is called upon to absorb aggression and anger from the very person he or she seeks to usher into God's presence.

Again, John Wesley models this grace. His interaction with his mentorees was open and reciprocal. Both parties could speak without reserve and without disguise.

When Wesley's harsh words about certain mystical writers offended Henry Brooke, the latter confronted Wesley with his "excess." Wesley responded to Brook in these words.

> Dear Harry,
>
> Your letter gave me pleasure and pain too. It gave me pleasure because it was written in a mild and loving spirit; and it gave me pain because I found I had pained you whom I so tenderly love and esteem. But I shall do it no more; I sincerely thank you for your kind reproof; it is a precious balm—and will, I trust, in the hands of the Great Physician, be a means of healing my sickness. I am so sensible of your real friendship herein that I cannot write without tears. The words you mention were too strong and they will no more fall from my mouth.
>
> My dear Harry, cease not to pray for your obliged and affectionate brother.
>
> John Wesley[24]

In responding to his banker friend and critic, Ebenezer Blackwell, Wesley said: "You do well to warn me against 'popularity, a thirst of power and applause, . . . against an affected humility, against sparing from myself to give to others from no other motive than ostentation.' I am not conscious to myself that this is my case. However, the warning is always friendly . . . always seasonable, considering how deceitful my heart is and how many the enemies that surround me."[25]

6. *Successful faith mentors practice self-giving love.* Faith mentors love others enough to give a lot of their time and energy helping someone else's dreams come true. Sondra Matthaei reports how "Kathy" found a mentor whom she says "is my vision keeper. He holds my image in trust like a jewel and gives it to me when I need it. But he holds it for me because it is his vision for me, too. This image of vision keeper has become my model of ministry."[26]

He holds my image in trust like a jewel and gives it to me when I need it.

Most effective faith mentors are marked by a self-giving love that expresses itself in uncommon affection. The first quality one notices in Wesley's letters is his unabashed love and affection for his correspondents. His language sounds a lot like Paul's words to the Thessalonians: "With such yearning love we chose to impart to you not only the gospel of God but our very selves, so dear had you become to us" (1 Thess. 2:8, NEB).

To Peggy Dale, Wesley says, "I thought it was hardly possible for me to love you better than I did . . . But your artless, simple, undisguised affection exceedingly increased mine."[27]

Miss Clarkson is told: "I love you because I believe you are upright of heart and because you are a child of affliction."[28] "I have always loved you since I knew you," Wesley tells to Mrs. Knapp, "but lately more than ever, because I believe you are more devoted to God and more athirst for his whole image."[29]

Hundreds of such expressions of uncommon affection punctuate Wesley's letters of spiritual guidance.

"Self-giving love frees persons to see themselves in new ways, to cope with threatening feelings, and to test new behaviors. Faith mentors incarnate God's love in nonpossessive ways."[30]

THE DOG DID NOT DIE

"What has given you the most satisfaction, inspiration, or pleasure during the last year?" With this question, I opened a seminar attended by 20 pastors. I gave them a moment to think about the question, and then I began to call for their responses. The third minister I called on said, "I can't think of one thing in those categories that happened to me. It's been another year of personal and professional losses. Come back to me later—maybe I can think of something."

I went on around the circle and eventually came back to him as he had invited me to do. This time he said, "The only thing that I can think of that comes close to satisfaction or pleasure is that my dog didn't die." I must have looked at him strangly, so he quickly explained: "I've had him for nine years. He was sick when I had to go away on a trip. I was sure he would die while I was gone. But when I got back, my dog hadn't died."

During a break, I asked him if he had a "soul friend," a person outside his family to whom he could talk "without reserve and without disguise." Like so many other ministers, he had no one—no one "wing to wing and oar to oar."

▶ For Personal Action and Reflection ◀

1. Evaluating Ideas
The main ideas emphasized in this chapter include the following. Review them and circle the one idea that is most important to you right now.

A. Every Christian needs someone to talk to about life's deepest concerns, but many have no such friend.

B. John Wesley hands us a great model for doing spiritual guidance.

C. Definitions and qualities of faith mentors and soul friends.

D. A faith mentor or spiritual friend may influence many areas of life, not just the practice of the spiritual life.

E. A good faith mentor or spiritual friend is "God's usher"—a person who can usher us into the presence of God and move us closer to Him.

2. The Faces Behind the Characteristics

A. In chap. 14, the qualities or characteristics of those persons whom God uses as one-to-one faith mentors or spiritual friends are discussed. (See *What Does a Faith Mentor Look Like?*)

A faith mentor:

—*is sensitive about relationships*
—*embodies the grace of God*
—*knows how to listen with acceptance and respect*
—*can often discern the moving of God's Spirit*
—*has the quality of vulnerable openness*
—*practices self-giving love*

B. Review what the book has to say about the foregoing qualities. Then, as you think about each of the qualities, write down the name of someone who demonstrates that quality. Give particular attention to persons who have exercised those gifts in your behalf. Take time to pray for all the persons whose faces appear when you think of the various faith mentoring qualities. Why not write them notes or give them a call and tell them that they are in your prayers of thanksgiving?

C. On a scale of 1-10 (with 1 being perfect and 10 being awful), how would you rate yourself when it comes to possessing and practicing the qualities of good faith mentors and spiritual friends? Consider each quality carefully—no false humility. Take a close look at the gifts you have for serving other Christians.

3. Into the Word

The Bible lesson for this chapter is 1 Thessalonians 2 and 3. Study these chapters with the list of qualities for faith

mentors in mind. Take care to note and list the qualities noted in the book which Paul demonstrates in chapters 2 and 3
of 1 Thessalonians.

For example, Paul *practices self-giving love* according to
2:8, which reads: "With such yearning love we chose to impart to you not only the gospel of God but our very selves, so
dear had you become to us" (NEB). You will be surprised to
find how well Paul fits the profile for faith mentors as found
in chap. 14.

4. For Your Journal

As you make your entries in your spiritual life journal this
week, create a dialogue with the author of this chapter. Tell
the author what you liked best and least about the chapter.
List any further questions you have for him. Let the author
know what changes you would make if you were assigned to
rewrite this chapter. Also, list any insights gained and any
spiritual progress you have made as you studied this chapter.

> What is our hope, our joy, our crown of exultation, in
> the presence of our Lord Jesus at his advent? Is it not
> indeed you? Yes, you are our glory and joy
> (1 Thess. 2:19-20).[1]

15

Together We Can Make It: The New Look of Faith Mentors

Dante's classic *The Divine Comedy* is probably the most finely crafted story ever written about mentoring. In it, Dante is called to make a journey to love and heaven. His beloved Beatrice is in heaven, and Dante hopes to land on the blissful shore where he will be reunited with the love of his life and live eternally in God's presence.

Love and heaven, however, are not easily attained. To get there, Dante must journey through hell and purgatory (Dante was a Catholic living before the Protestant Reformation during the years 1265-1321). "Midway through the journey of life," the story begins, Dante is lost in a foreboding forest where he is being chased by ferocious animals. He is terrified and cannot find his way out of the woods. When he has abandoned all hope, Virgil, the Roman poet, appears to help Dante on his journey. What happens after that is the classic illustration of the mentor-protégé relationship.

Virgil provides the vision for the journey. He convinces Dante that he is an envoy from Beatrice, who awaits him in heaven. Virgil has already been through hell; therefore, he knows the territory. He fills all the mentoring roles as he urges Dante not to quit, explains mysteries, points the way, guides through treacherous terrain, translates arcane codes, protects from harm, calms vicious beasts, removes obstacles, and constantly encourages Dante. At one point, Virgil picks up the mentoree, Dante, as he would a child and plummets down a rocky embankment to escape a band of evil spirits.

Virgil, the mentor, brings Dante to the very pit of hell, where the Beast, Satan sits. Symbolic of facing one's own "dark side," Dante looks on the devil himself. But hanging onto Virgil's neck, he escapes.

The next part of the journey is the trek through purgatory—less threatening than hell itself. Having gained savvy and experience by his journey through hell, Dante now begins to walk by the side of Virgil instead of following behind him. The relationship between the two travelers moves toward equality. In Hell, Virgil was the protecting authority. Now he becomes friend and adviser.

As the journey nears heaven, Virgil takes his leave. He cannot lead Dante further. And, as in many mentoring relationships, the one mentored moves beyond the vision and experience of the mentor. At the brink of heaven, Virgil gives his last blessing and encouragement: "Free, upright and whole is thy will . . . therefore over thyself I crown . . . thee."

In accounts of relationships like those of Virgil and Dante, Mentor and Odysseus, and Elijah and Elisha, we find rich and brilliant insights into faith mentoring. This is the evangelism of the 21st century. Over the last several decades, Christians have taken all sorts of training and spared no effort at trying to master the knack of winning strangers to Christ in airplanes, on the street, and on the job. The evangelism champ was the one who could win a soul between the salads and the desserts in the cafeteria.

Such things we pursued while our children and others already connected to the church slipped unnoticed out the back door. But we have learned our lesson—the quick-fix gospel doesn't work. If we are going to properly evangelize, we must spend *more* time with *fewer* people. That means that we must become intentional about faith mentoring. That is to say, we shall not leave mentoring to chance, but engage in faith mentoring on purpose.

This story shows us some of the ways faith mentors work. Actually, their roles are as varied as the wide scope of human needs.

I have stood mentorless at more than one crossroad, but in most of life's tough decisions and crucial turning points, God, in His grace, has put a mentor at my elbow. If I have achieved anything worthwhile it has been due to enabling mentors in both my personal and professional life. They have been there, believing in me, encouraging me, giving me opportunities, and sometimes caring enough to confront. I started to put here a list of names of persons who have facilitated my dreams and visions. But while I am proud of them, they may not want to take credit for any of my antics. So in kindness I shall let those pastors, teachers, supervisors, colleagues, and family members who have mentored me remain anonymous for now.

THE ROLES OF FAITH MENTORS

Sondra Matthaei identifies seven roles of the faith mentor: guide, coach, model, sponsor, advocate, guarantor, and mediator. Let us glance briefly at these roles as they appear in life and in 1 Thessalonians.

1. Guide

The faith mentor is like a guide who has traveled this road before. He or she knows what lies ahead in terms of hazards, challenges, and achievements. The faith mentor guide points the way like an experienced trail scout.

A faith mentor guide does not operate alone in spiritual matters. We cannot separate our religious devotion from the rest of life. Therefore, decisions about education, marriage, finances, and careers are grist for dialogue with a faith mentor guide.

My friend, Milton, has an important job with a large corporation. Over the last dozen years of our relationship, he has lost four or five assistants. His most recently lost assistant wrote him this note:

Dear Milton:
> Thanks for your generosity toward me when I left. I hated to leave, but the company offered me a job I couldn't refuse. I never thought I would ever get a job like this. I know I owe a lot to you. You taught me so much.
> I will never forget my days in your department.

> All the best,
> Jim

When I commented on the parade of assistants who had left him, Milton simply said, "They all went on to bigger and better things. You know, part of my job description is to make sure that my subordinates succeed. When they do, I feel like it's payday."

> **A mentor-coach makes us watch the game films, makes us watch our mistakes in painful slow motion. That's accountability.**

When Timothy returned with the good report about the Thessalonica Christians, Paul, their mentor, felt like it was payday too. He wrote to them, "What is our hope, our joy, our crown of exultation in the presence of our Lord Jesus at his advent? Is it not indeed you? Yes, you are our glory and joy" (1 Thess. 2:19-20).[2]

Milton, the business mentor, teaches us another important point about mentoring. The mentor-protégé or mentor-mentoree relationship does not usually last for a lifetime. In the nature of things, the mentoree will often "grow past" the mentor. Sometimes the dissolution of the relationship is tense, even explosive. The good mentor knows when to let go. The good coach does not turn bitter when his player graduates.

Again we find an example in John Wesley's life. William Law, author of *A Serious Call to the Devout and Holy Life*, nurtured Wesley in holiness, but when Wesley's own understanding and vision of the holy life outstripped Law's, Wesley all but renounced him. Sometimes the function of a faith mentor is to put your feet on his shoulders so you can reach higher than the mentor himself can ever reach.

A friend of mine watched a mentoree turn his back and walk away from him. His response was classic: "Teach a kid to fiddle and he's liable to become a violinist."

2. Coach

Another important role of the faith mentor is that of coach. A coach instructs us in the rules of the game, helps us develop skills, encourages us when the going gets rough, and holds us accountable for our performance.

Paul speaks as an instructor-coach when he tells the Thessalonians that he deeply desires to see them face-to-face so that he can "perfect that which is lacking in their faith" (see 1 Thess. 3:10).

I played football in high school. I remember that experience with positive feelings—except when Coach Brown would yank me out of the game and hold me accountable for a missed tackle or dropped pass. As unpleasant as it is, we all need mentors who will hold us accountable.

The mentor-coach makes us watch the game films. He or she shows us what we did right, and what we did wrong—in painful slow motion. The mentor-coach teaches us new skills, skills we may not even know we need until we watch the game films.

Paul, the faith mentor, hoped to impart skills of prayer (5:17), thanksgiving (v. 18) abstaining from evil (v. 22); encouraging and comforting one another (4:18; 5:11), self-control (4:3-5), and brotherly love (3:12). He wanted to equip them all with the breastplate of faith and love, the helmet of salvation, and the protection of sobriety and alertness (5:4-8).

In sports, it is often the coach who won't let you give up when the going gets tough. When Ann Bolton was overwhelmed with sorrow and suffering, her mentor-coach wrote, "It seems good to our Lord to try you as by fire . . . look up to Him that loves you. Tell Him as a little child all your wants. Look up . . . He hears the cry of your heart."[3]

When Jane Hilton, a new Christian under Wesley's mentoring, was devastated by a withering temptation, he wrote to her, "Christ is yours; and He is wiser and stronger than all the powers of hell. Hang upon Him . . . lean on Him with the whole weight of your soul."[4] Her spiritual coach would not let her give up.

Teach a kid to fiddle and he's liable to become a violinist.

In much the same manner, Paul writes to the Thessalonian believers. When they and their leaders, Jason and Aristarchus, turned Christian, the local citizenry turned on them. They hired the services of the biggest "rent-a-mob" agency in Greece and ran Paul out of town and arrested Jason and Aristarchus.

Coach Paul would not let them give up, even in the face of murderous persecution. Though he could not get into town to see them, he sent Timothy (whom the persecutors would not know) into the huddle with instructions about what play to run.

Paul gave them this speech at halftime in a very tough game. "[I want] to establish you firmly and encourage you . . . so that no one should be perturbed in the midst of these afflictions. You know yourselves that we are appointed for this. Indeed . . . we warned you that we are bound to suffer affliction, even as it has turned out" (1 Thess. 3:2-4).[5]

I remember my football coach giving us that kind of speech. He would say, "I never told you it was going to be easy! The problem with you guys is that you want to wear a football uniform, but you don't want to play football. I'm looking for 11 men who want to play *football* in the second half! Yes, we are behind. But it's way too soon to give up!"

How fortunate is the Christian who has a spiritual friend or a faith mentor who will give him or her such a speech when the going gets tough!

We need to note one last thing about a coach. He or she can give speeches, show game films, teach skills—but the coach cannot and should not play the game for you. A spiritual friend or a faith mentor cannot make your tough decisions for you, cannot take over your problems and solve them. He or she cannot thrash all your enemies, take your final exams, or protect you from every blizzard. Rather, your spiritual coach remains on the sideline, encouraging, challenging, and urging you on in your upward quest on the highway of holiness.

3. Model

The person searching for a spiritual friend or faith mentor is looking for a living example, a model of the holy life. He or she is looking for someone "to be like." Every new believer needs a trustworthy model who demonstrates the grace of God in spirituality, in relationships, and in making meaning of life.

The Thessalonians found such a model in Paul and his company of missionaries. Paul was not afraid to take the *model* role, either. He wrote, "You . . . know what kind of persons we were among you for your sakes . . . You became imitators of us and of the Lord, when you accepted the word" (1:5-6).[6] Later in the same letter, Paul says, "You are witnesses, and so is God, how devout, just and blameless our behavior was" (2:10).[7]

A model is, according to Sondra Matthaei, a "respected person who journeys with us, a living example of spirituality, lifestyle, values, sharing life experiences, vocation, intimacy, femininity/masculinity, and honesty."[8]

Laurent Daloz notes that as we observe our models, we need to realize that in the end we do not slavishly try "to become **like** them, but . . . more fully ourselves **through** them."[9]

Faith mentors are often journeymen Christians who permit apprentice Christians "to look over their shoulders as they both attempt to live as Christians."[10] When we observe that Christianity is better *caught* than *taught,* we affirm our belief that Christian role models are even more important than a catechism classroom.

> **Young people need trustworthy
> adult models who give wordless
> guarantees to the fact that
> adulthood is a good place to be.**

4. Sponsor

Sometimes faith mentoring takes on the *sponsor* role. One Los Angeles church has formalized the sponsor role. Each young person seeking to be "confirmed" is assigned a sponsor, whose role is printed for all to see:

a. A model of how a *person* of faith lives in today's world.

b. A *friend* who knows the candidate and can witness to the maturing faith of the candidate before the community.

c. A *guide* confidant and listener.

d. A *learner* who is interested in his or her own growth as he or she walks the faith journey with the candidate.

e. One who will . . . invite the candidate into fuller participation in parish life and service.[11]

Paul was a sponsor-mentor to the new believers at Thessalonica. "We . . . were gentle among you, like a nurse cherishing her own children. Such was our affection . . . It is life to us, if you stand fast in the Lord" (2:7-8; 3:8).[12]

In what ways would a designated sponsor in the church have helped you as a young person or a new Christian?

5. Advocate

Each pilgrim on the highway of holiness at one time or another needs a spiritual friend who can become an advocate. Family and friends and fellow Christians may not understand and may lose faith in you. But an advocate goes to bat for you, believes in you, stands with you, pleads your case, and affirms you. An advocate supports your honest search for meaning, truth, and identity, showing patience and giving you space to grow.

The Thessalonian believers found such an advocate in Paul who stood up for them as if they were his own children. "We treated each one of you," he wrote, "as a father would treat his own children. Thus we exhorted you, encouraged you" (2:11-12).[13]

6. Guarantor

Ross Snyder, David Ng, Sondra Matthaei, and William Myers speak of the faith mentor as *guarantor*.[14] The idea of guarantor fits faith mentoring of the journeyman-apprentice, mature-inexperienced, senior-junior, or old-young type relationships.

There are plenty of fake guarantors around, as Stephen Crane points out:

> A learned man came to me once.
> He said, "I know the way—come,"
> And I was overjoyed at this.
> Together we hastened,
> Soon, too soon, were we
> Where my eyes were useless,
> And I knew not the ways of my feet.
> I clung to the hand of my friend;
> But at last he cried, "I am lost."[15]

Youth need trustworthy models who "incarnate *adult-*

ness in ways that encourage young people to grow. In this way, they *guarantee* the fact that adulthood will be a good place to be."[16]

Such guarantors are a working models of "the next step." They are adults who are "living the becoming future now." The faith mentor implies to observing youth that the future is worth facing, that authentic faith in God makes it so.[17]

Of course, Jesus Christ is the greatest Guarantor of all. And He is the model for all faith mentor guarantors. Paul and the Thessalonians found Jesus Christ, whose grace, gospel, death, and resurrection make life, even with murderous persecution, worth living.

7. Mediator

One of the basic Protestant principles is "the priesthood of all believers." To modern Americans, that simply means that they can pray directly to God without having to go through a priest. But that is only part of the meaning of the priesthood of all believers. The neglected meaning has to do with the fact that all ordinary Christians can become priests to one another. That's one way to describe the mutual service that faith mentors and soul friends give to each other. It is a ministry of mediation.

Therefore, one of the roles of a faith mentor is that of a mediator, a person who brings together persons and possibilities. A priest is to bring God and the people together. Jesus, our Great High Priest and Mediator, brings us into contact with God's saving and sanctifying grace.

A human faith mentor can mediate love, grace, self-knowledge, and discernment of the will of God, as well as acceptance, assurance, and a sense of direction in life. A faith mediator can mediate between a painful past and a promise-filled future in the sunshine of God's redeeming love. A soul friend can become a mediating bridge that connects what we have been to what we can be.

Paul saw the dreams of the new believers in Thessalonica. As a mediator-mentor, he sought to lead them to the highway of holiness. His deepest wish for their future is seen in his two prayers for them in chapters 3 and 5. "May our God and Father himself and our Lord Jesus . . . establish your hearts blameless in holiness" (3:11, 13).[18] In the climactic closing section of the Epistle, Paul sums up his heart's desire for the Thessalonian believers in a benedictory prayer. "May the God of peace himself sanctify you completely, and may your spirit and soul and body be preserved . . . free from blame. He who calls you is faithful; he will do it" (5:23-24).[19]

> **Being a soul friend or faith mentor
> is to live out the Protestant
> principle of the priesthood
> of all believers.**

The faith mentor-mediator brings the mentoree's personal story and religious experience into contact with the heart of the Christian faith as taught in the Bible and Christian tradition. The mediator-mentor is, according to James Fowler, involved in "an ongoing process . . . through which people (or a group) gradually bring the lived story of their lives into congruence with the core story of the Christian faith."[20] Thus, an effective faith mentor needs to *know* the core beliefs of the Christian faith, and he or she must *know* the Bible. Edward Sellner asserts that a mentor should be "something of a scholar," who continually reflects on experience and faith and God. "This faith-seeking understanding—Anselm's definition of theology—presupposes a knowledge of Christian traditions, the scripture . . . [and] culture."[21]

The trustworthy mediator-mentor also brings the mentoree's personal faith journey and religious experiences into dynamic relationship with a community of faith. Beware of the spiritual guide who does not form a bridge between the biblical core of the Christian faith. Beware of the spiritual guide who does not lead you to the Church, the called-out community of faith.

We have looked at the qualities and roles of faith mentors and spiritual friends. Such persons seem bigger than life. About the only thing we haven't cataloged about them is the wing span of these angels.

"It would be nice to have a faith mentor," you may be saying, "but an ordinary person like me could never become one." You could say that, but you would be wrong.

No human mentor can possess all the qualities or fill all the roles that have been cited. Nevertheless, most of us can serve as faith mentors or spiritual friends to someone at some time.

You look at your busy schedule and sigh, "How could I ever find time to be a mentor or soul friend?" While it is true that Christians must spend more time with fewer people, nurturing relationships do not necessarily dominate your time. Many mentoring relationships are of short duration, some as short as a week, a day, an hour.

THE ORIGINAL MENTOR

Now that we have dealt with mentors and mentoring for many pages, it may be time to think about where the original word *mentor* came from. Mentor is a character who inhabits the Greek epics like the *Iliad* and the *Odyssey*. He was a good and wise man whose counsel was treasured. He was the boyhood friend of Odysseus. In his long journey home, Odysseus receives counsel from the absent Mentor by way of Athena, the goddess of wisdom, who comes to Odysseus in the form of Mentor.

Mentor is assigned to the task of looking after Odysseus' son, Telemachus. In the son's search for his father, Mentor guides him. Again, it is Athena who comes to Telemachus in Mentor's form to give advice. "Thus, Mentor is both male and female, mortal and immortal . . . Wisdom personified."[22]

Athena, in the form of Mentor, helps the son, father,

and grandfather recapture the heritage that is theirs. Athena herself is described as "self-confident, courageous, clear-eyed, strong, intelligent . . . judicious and fair." She is also called "soul maker" and "soul giver."[23]

Through the centuries, those interested in "making souls" and transmitting a spiritual heritage have found in this classic story a helpful model of what we now call faith mentors.

▶ For Personal Action and Reflection ◀

1. Let Me Tell You How I Feel . . .

Which of the following describes the feelings you had while reading chap. 15? Check all that apply and think about why you felt that way.

    A. I wish I'd known that back when . . .
    B. Wow, what a wonderful idea!
    C. Ho-hum.
    D. There's hope for me.
    E. I could do that.
    F. That's really scary.
    G. What a relief!
    H. Why hasn't this happened to me?
    I. "Thank You, Lord, for . . ."
    J. Rejoice, again I say rejoice.
    K. That feels like sunshine.
    L. How depressing!
    M. Other

2. Understanding Concepts

In chap. 15, seven roles for faith mentors are presented. Review those roles, making sure you understand each one and how each of the roles is in some way different from the others. In the space provided, write one statement that, for you, is the "key" idea about this role.

    A. Guide:

B. Coach:

C. Model:

D. Sponsor:

E. Advocate:

F. Guarantor:

G. Mediator:

Look over the list and your comments and think about the following questions: (1) Which of these roles has *someone* filled for me? (2) Which of these roles has *no one* filled for me? (3) Which of these roles should I be filling for someone else? Be specific—give names.

3. Back to the Bible

The following scripture passages are quoted in chap. 15. Turn to 1 Thessalonians in your Bible and read them again. Read them prayerfully, asking the Holy Spirit to speak to your open heart. You are not studying for an exam, analyzing Greek words, or trying to make a list—you are just opening your mind and heart to whatever the Spirit may want to say or do as you read and meditate. Here are the passages: 1 Thess. 2:7-12; 3:8, 11-13; 4:3-5, 18; 5:17-18, 22-24.

4. For Your Journal

A. From the above-listed scripture passages, select a verse to memorize. Write it in your journal. Study it. Put it on the back of your business card, or on a slip of paper and carry it this week in your purse or wallet. Repeat the verse as the table grace at each meal.

B. Review the section in chap. 15 that deals with the faith mentor as coach. Notice that one of the things a coach does is to make us watch the game films as he or she points out what we did best and what we did poorly. Be your own coach. Select one area of the holy life you have been working on lately. In your mind, prayerfully run the "game film." In your journal, write a heading "Coach's Comments." Then list advisements, encouragements, and corrections. Come back to read this part of your journal next week to see how you are doing in carrying out the "Coach's Comments."

C. A prayer to make your own (A personalized paraphrase of 1 Thess. 5:23):

May God himself, the God of peace
  Make me holy in every part,
Sanctifying me through and through,
And keeping me sound in spirit, soul, and body,
Holy and clean, ready for the coming of our Lord Jesus
  Christ.

Amen

Our killing schedules, our sleepiness in the morning, and our weariness at night make family worship the last spiritual discipline implemented and the first to be neglected.

16

Spiritual Nurture in the Family

My daughter, the sociologist, was invited to teach a series on the family to a large adult Sunday School class. She dusted off her lecture notes and the textbooks she used to teach a college class. She distributed a questionnaire, however, to find what the felt needs were. The number one need cited by the class members had nothing to do with social theory relating to marriage or to parenting skills. They simply asked, "Can you teach us how to have family devotions?"

She ended up sharing with them John Wesley's plan for family worship. Those of us who bear the banner of our Wesleyan heritage may have proven ourselves to be quite "un-Wesleyan" by our failure to perfect family religion.

While examining John Wesley's small groups, we must not forget one of the most important of them—the family. Societies, classes, bands, and soul friends were important to Wesley, but so was family religion. Wesley assured his people that they would prove Martin Luther right if they neglected spiritual formation in the family. Luther had observed that revivals of religion lasted 30 years, that is, one generation. Wesley and his preachers worked hard to make sure that Christian education and the practice of devotion were a normal part of family life.

Traveling and local preachers were charged with the responsibility of helping parents with spiritual formation in the home. The preacher himself was to teach both parents and children in their homes. A preacher seeking admittance to the conference was confronted with: "Will you diligently and earnestly instruct the children and visit from house to house?"[1] At another time, Wesley challenged his preachers with this question: "For what avails preaching alone, though we preach like angels? We must, yea every travelling Preacher must, instruct them from house to house."[2]

Wesley armed the preachers and parents with published materials for spiritual formation in the home. He wrote a book of 200 Bible studies for children called *Lessons for Children*. This book was used in Methodist schools as well as in the home. Wesley provided a book of 58 lessons on Christian living, called *Instructions for Children*.

John Wesley urged parents to make every Thursday evening "children's night."

A number of other books were reprinted and used with families and children. Charles Wesley also published at least one book of hymns for children.

One book that was to be used daily in the home was *A Collection of Prayers for Families*. This document, issued several times during Wesley's ministry, contained family prayers for morning and evening for each day of the week. Wesley also provided a book called *Prayers for Children*.

Parents were to take the spiritual formation of their children seriously. Wesley taught them that their children were "immortal spirits whom God hath, for a time, entrusted to your care." And this He has done "that you may train them up in all holiness."[3]

Preaching from the text, "as for me and my house, we will serve the Lord" (Josh. 24:15), Wesley told parents that they must restrain their yet unconverted children through *advice, persuasion,* and *correction.* Correction included corporal punishment, but Wesley reminded them that this should be used only as a last resort. "And even then you should take the utmost care to avoid the very appearance of passion. Whatever is done should be done with mildness; nay, indeed, with kindness too."[4]

Wesley declared that those who tried to thrash their children into heaven should not think it strange "if religion stunk in the nostrils of those that were so educated. They will naturally look upon it as an austere, melancholy thing."[5]

To *advice, persuasion,* and *correction,* the Christian parent was to add *instruction.* This instruction was to be done *early, frequently,* and *patiently.*[6]

The parents were to see to it that the child had and took time "every day for reading, meditation, and prayer."[7] Family devotions were to be seriously and solemnly performed every day, twice a day, if possible.

Besides this, Thursday evening was to be set aside for catechizing the children. It had been the night Susanna set aside to give direct attention to her son, John. John never forgot those precious sessions. Susanna gave birth to 19 children, 11 of which survived infancy. She herself was the 25th child of her father. As busy as she was, she faithfully taught her children in groups and one-on-one. One of John Wesley's most poignant letters to his mother is a request that she pray for him on Thursday nights. John was a middle-aged man with ecclesiastical duties and demands from the societies all over England and Ireland weighing him down. He thought he could make it if he knew that on every Thursday, at least, Susanna was praying for him as she had formerly prayed with him as a child. It is no wonder that he urged every Methodist family to make every Thursday evening "children's night."

Saturday night was to be special too. On Saturdays, each child was to recite and report what he or she had learned that week.

FAMILY WORSHIP

Of particular interest was Wesley's insightful plan for family worship. In order to help parents who had little or no experience with such things, he set a precise order for family worship. The family gathered, and a short prayer opened the session. This was followed by psalm singing. Next came Bible study. The passage was read aloud by a parent. Following the reading, one parent explained the passage. Then the children were to explain the passage back to the parents in their own words. This method is ingenious educationally. It requires the parents to study the passage thoroughly enough to explain it so a child can understand. Further, it provides opportunity to check the child's grasp of the lesson when the child attempts to reexplain the passage.

> **No matter how unpleasant or disobedient the child had been that day, the parental blessing was never to be denied.**

After the Bible study came prayer. It started with a written prayer from *A Collection of Prayers for Families.* This was to be followed by appropriate extemporary prayer, which included prayer for each family member. Then came the singing of the doxology, and the pronouncement of a benediction by a parent, usually the father.

This was followed by one of the most important parts of this spiritual formation practice. Each child was to ask for a blessing. In response, father or mother laid hands on the child's head and blessed the child in Jesus' name. Wesley warned parents that no matter how unpleasant or disobedient the child had been that day, under no circumstance was this blessing to be denied.[8]

Imagine what it would mean to a child to be blessed in the name of Jesus by his or her parents every day. Would it not do more for the generation gap than even the sagacious counsel of Dr. Spock?

Perhaps the most "transferable" part of Wesley's system for spiritual formation in the family is his plan for family worship. Following is a contemporized version that you might wish to try in your own family or in a small group. I have used this exercise with gracious results in small groups and workshops on spiritual formation.

A WESLEYAN SERVICE OF FAMILY WORSHIP

A Short Prayer

Use extemporary prayer, or these words from Wesley's family prayers for Sunday:

> Almighty and eternal God, we desire to praise thy holy name
> . . . how great was thy love to the sinful sons of men! . . . Compose
> our spirits to a quiet and steady dependence on thy good providence.[9]

Psalm Singing

Use a hymn or gospel song if psalm singing is too much of a challenge for your family. If you like challenges, try singing this excerpt from Psalm 103.

> As a father pities his children,
> So the Lord pities them who fear Him.
> For He knows our frame;
> He remembers that we are dust.
>
> The mercy of the Lord is
> From everlasting to everlasting . . .
> To such as keep His covenant,
> And to those who remember His commandments.
>
> —Ps. 103:13-14, 17-18, NKJV

Bible Study

A. Select a passage for study, or use Psalm 103.
B. Parents read and explain the passage.
Cite the basic teaching of the passage. Use the folowing set of inquiry questions if you wish.
What does this passage teach us about God? About Christ? About humankind?
Is there a command to obey?
Is there a sin to avoid?
Is there a timeless truth to be understood?
Is there a promise to claim?
Is there a prayer I could make my own?
C. Children explain the passage back to the parents. Remember: children deal best with concrete ideas. Help them with examples in everyday life that explain the biblical concepts.

Prayer

Start by reading together one of the prayers used by Wesley. Be sure to explain the prayers to the family. Mere recital of words not understood is not very helpful.

(1) *Almighty God, unto whom all hearts are open, all desires known, and from whom no secrets are hid; cleanse the thoughts of our hearts by the inspiration of Thy Holy Spirit, that we may perfectly love Thee, and worthily magnify Thy holy name through Christ our Lord. Amen.*[10]

(2) *O Lord, increase in us faith and devotion; give us humility and propriety, patience in adversity, and continual joy in the Holy Ghost.*

Give us modesty in our countenance, composure in our behavior, wisdom in our speech, holiness in our actions. Let thy mercy cleanse us from all our sins, and confirm us in all righteousness.[11]

(3) *Sing the Doxology together.*

(4) *The Benediction.* (Given by father or mother)

Use a benediction of your own, a Bible verse or this benedictory prayer from John Wesley.

Pardon, O gracious Jesus, what we have been.
With all thy holy discipline correct what we are.
Order by thy providence what we shall be,
And in the end crown all thy gifts. Amen.[12]

(5) *The Blessing:*

Each child shall say, "Father (mother), bless me in Jesus' name."

Parental Response (never to be refused). "___(name)___, I *bless you in the name of Jesus who loves you and gave His life for you. May His forgiveness, grace, and peace be yours this day/night, and every day of your life.*"[13]

With so many varied living arrangements in today's society, even the term *family* has varied meanings. Millions live alone, millions more live with same-gender housemates. In addition, we have one-parent families, fragmented families, blended families, intergenerational families (absent parent with grandparents raising grandchildren), and the traditional family. Therefore, the family as the arena for spiritual formation has varied meanings. Nevertheless, most Christians have familylike relationships with somebody. This natural grouping must not be neglected as an arena for spiritual formation.

Family worship is an important but fragile thing. It is the hardest thing to schedule. It seems hard to get the whole family together for a meal, let alone a worship time. Too many of us, including the children, *especially the children*, have so many activities. Even when we try to plan our schedules, our killing schedules, our sleepiness in the morning, and our weariness at night make family worship the last spiritual discipline implemented and the first to be neglected.

When I was a child growing up in Missouri, my father and mother conducted family worship six nights a week. We did not have family worship on Sundays. Mom and Dad figured that Sunday School and two worship or evangelistic services was all the religion a kid could cope with in one day.

But somewhere along the way we stopped having family devotions. After I left home and went to college and seminary and had become a young pastor, I asked my father one day why we stopped having family devotions. I was not prepared for his answer. "Well, it was this way, son. When you got to be about 15, you became so cynical and surly that Mom and I didn't have the heart to keep trying to make family devotions work. Your attitude just ruined it for the younger children."

Yes, indeed, family worship is important—and it is a fragile thing. And I am glad our Lord is a God of forgiving grace.

It is God's plan to use our fellow Christians as His assistants in helping us live the holy life. He works through our families, through faith mentors, spiritual friends, face-to-face groups, and nurturing congregations. "The Lord has given us to each other to strengthen each other's hands."

▶ For Personal Action and Reflection ◀

1. Bible Study
   A. Read Eph. 5:21—6:4
   B. A quiz on what family members need from each other. According to this passage:
   (1) What *wives* need from *husbands* is—
       (a) obedience *(b)* love *(c)* encouragement
   (2) What *husbands* need from *wives* is—
       (a) respect *(b)* love *(c)* sexual comforts
   (3) What *husbands* and *wives* need to offer each other is (see v. 21)—
       (a) fair treatment *(b)* mutual submission *(c)* money
   (4) What *children* need from *parents* is—
       (a) discipline *(b)* instruction *(c)* patient understanding
   (5) What *children* should give their *parents* is—
       (a) obedience *(b)* honor *(c)* back talk

2. Family Worship
   Review "A Wesleyan Service of Family Worship." Adapt it for use with your own family. Don't be discouraged if it feels awkward at first. Keep using this general structure for several family worship times.

PART IV

Finding Ways to Serve Others on Our Journey

. . . redemptive action in our world.

♦

If any man will come after me, let him deny himself, and take up his cross daily, and follow me
(Luke 9:23, KJV).

♦

We do not acknowledge him to have one grain of faith who is not continually doing good, who is not willing to spend and be spent in doing all good, as he has opportunity, to all men.
—John Wesley, *The Letters of the Rev. John Wesley, A.M.*

♦

A spirituality that does not lead to active ministry becomes an indulgent preoccupation with self, and therefore grieves the Holy Spirit and violates the presence of the indwelling Christ.
—Maxie Dunnam, *Alive in Christ*

♦

Show me your faith apart from your works, and I by my works will show you my faith
(James 2:18, RSV).

Introduction to Part IV
FINAL EXAM

Now we get down to the nitty gritty—
   To the test of the pudding—
   To the final exam!
   That test asks you point blank, "Does your spirituality produce self-sacrificing Christian service?" If Christ has been formed in you, you will, like Christ, lay down your life in service to God and the people for whom He died.

You see, you may admire Christ, love Him with a sentimental attachment, wish to have His smile, His guidance, and treasure His presence. You may even prize moments of meditation and enjoy the study of the Bible. You may enjoy the comforts of public worship, the encouragement of a Christian support group—and still fail the final exam, still hold back from full self-surrender, from sacrificial service.

Unless the exercise of the spiritual disciplines eventuate in loving service, they turn out to be—in your case— shallow exercises of halfway discipleship and misguided efforts of self-righteousness. And full self-surrender is the prelude to holy service.

The members of the writing team for this book have studied spiritual formation literature from every Christian century, from New Testament times up to the present. One thing discovered in every Christian generation is that the final gate through which the pilgrim must pass to enter the deeper life in God is self-surrender, self-denial, or self-donation, as it was called in the Middle Ages.

Mary Reuters, in *Formation Through Encounters of Ordinary Life,* searches for 1,182 pages for the key to the spiritual life. In the end, she concludes that the key to the holy life is self-surrender. It always has been and always will be. Even the most liberal writers on spirituality come to the same point. Matthew Fox, famous for his spirituality of ecstasy, agrees. His book, *Whee, We, Wee All the Way Home,* which features a pig with a flower in its mouth in a swing on the cover, coaches the reader that whatever feels good is spiritual, that we are closest to God in moments of ecstasy. The libertine is feeling great until Fox reaches the bottom line and tells them that true ecstasy comes when we transcend self-interest and serve others, particularly those in need.

Catholic and Protestant, conservative and liberal, Calvinistic or Arminian—the saints of all the Christian generations have discovered that the key to the holy life is self-surrender.

Like a choir in close harmony, they tell us that self-surrender is the prelude to service. And service is the one true test of spirituality. If Christ is formed in your heart, your hands will perform Christlike deeds.

In Part IV of this book you will read about how Christ gave His life away. You will encounter principles of Christian service as a spiritual discipline and you will bump into people who show us what Christian service looks like. This is dangerous ground. It could cost you your plans, your dreams—it could cost you your life. Jesus may call you to follow His example and give your life away—in fact, you can count on it.

The French are great cyclists and the Tour de France is the greatest bicycle race of all. If you watch the French team, you will notice the *domestique* (servant). He will not win the race. He is not intended to win. Yet mile after weary mile he pedals on. His job is to shield the top cyclist who will win the race. The *domestique* shields him from the wind, creates a draft in which the "star" cyclist will ride throughout the race. The *domestique* gets no trophy, no medal, no credit. The one whom he enabled throughout the race is crowned—and that is enough for the *domestique.* Holy service is all about becoming a *domestique* for Christ and our fellow travelers.

> There are plenty to follow our Lord half-way . . . They give up possessions, friends, honors, but it touches them too closely to disown themselves.
> —Meister Eckhart

17

Self-surrender: Prelude to Service

It is a long way down from anchoring television news to changing bedpans. This, however, was my basic training for holy service. It began in 1981. I had been covering the Iranian hostage crisis for KNBC news. After observing the faith of Pastor Earl and Hazel Lee, whose son was one of the 52 Americans taken hostage, I asked Jesus into my heart. A year later I stepped out of my career in journalism over a moral conviction and began sharing my testimony all over the country. Response to my conversion story was overwhelming. And yet the kudos of being a Christian "celebrity" could not fill a void in my soul. Something was seriously missing. And it took the honesty of a retired woman evangelist and a long walk to Calvary to find it!

I had no doubt that God had called me to full-time ministry. My goal was to come home and minister to the senior adults at Pasadena First Church of the Nazarene. Without delay, I enrolled in seminary courses to prepare for the work. Then I marched into Pastor Lee's office to reveal my detailed plans.

However, he was not sold on the idea. To my dumb-founded amazement he said, "No!"

"Why not?" I asked.

"You're not ready!" he replied.

"Well, then, how do I get ready?" I appealed.

He paused and gently said, "Pray."

I took Pastor Lee's response as a personal put-down and hastily left in a huff.

Within a few days I received a call from Rev. Estelle Crutcher, a retired elder in the church (and, incidentally, Pastor Lee's mother-in-law). In a nurturing tone, "Grandma" Crutcher said, "Dah'ling, I hear you are depressed. Why not come over and let's talk about it?"

Hungry for a sympathetic ear, I rushed over, not expecting a spiritual showdown.

"Dear," Grandma began, "Pastor Lee is not the real problem here. Your desire to work at the church is not the real problem either. It's your *ego. Crucify it!* And let the Holy Spirit cleanse and entirely sanctify you!"

The older woman's assessment stung my heart. I left speechless.

A few days later, a senior adult dying of cancer called the church requesting someone to come over and help clean her home. Pastor Lee shared her request. I picked up the church vacuum cleaner and set out to help. After all, I thought, I have nothing better to do.

Within a few weeks, the house-cleaning job evolved into nursing assistance, in which I turned, bathed, fed, and changed my new elderly friend. And as word of my new "calling" spread, there were more homes to clean, more invalids to serve.

One morning, while I was on my knees scrubbing a kitchen floor, it happened. Grandma Crutcher's powerful challenge about walking to Calvary and allowing my *all* to be crucified for Jesus began to take hold. I felt the Holy Spirit beckoning me to nail down my zeal, my vision for a job at the church *and* my critical spirit toward Pastor Lee.

Tears flowed as I poured out my heart for cleansing. All desires for a pastoral position were consumed by a passion to know and be like Jesus. At last my carnal appetite for titles and recognition was on the Cross. The Holy Spirit filled *and* set me free from having to live up to my own and everyone else's expectations.

From that moment on I could identify with Paul's proclamation in Gal. 2:20: "I have been crucified with Christ and I no longer live, but Christ lives in me" (NIV). For Paul, death with Christ was the only way to be freed from the enslavement of the law. All reliance on works for his salvation was severed. This death, however, was accompanied by new life. When Paul declares, "but Christ lives in me," he is saying the carnal ego in control of his life has been replaced by Christ.

> ## Be glad and eager to throw yourself headlong into His dear arms.
> —Hannah Whitall Smith
> *The Christian's Secret of a Happy Life*

At this point, you may be wondering why we are addressing the issues of self-surrender and sanctification again. The reason is simple. **Holy service begins and continues at the Cross.** Death to self-will opens the gates of our hearts to receive God's sanctifying grace and impart this grace in service to others. And this cleansing, healing, and helping grace will fill and flow through us as we *continually* identify with Christ's death and resurrection.

When Paul claimed, "I have been crucified with Christ," he was not referring to a one-time experience. The perfect tense in Greek emphasizes not only a completed act but also a continuing state. In other words, Paul is saying, "I have been, and still am, crucified with Christ." By remaining on the Cross, Paul's service for God was delivered from self-seeking, self-serving, and self-promotion. So it is with us. We cannot begin to serve Christ and serve like Him until we submit our all and die daily with Him. Calvary is where the victory comes, where sanctified service is born and sustained through the power of the Holy Spirit. The Spirit's infilling not only refreshes our desire to serve but also purifies our motives to serve.

Still, even the most holy and active servants must beware of temptation. Just as Jesus was tempted to save himself and come down from the Cross, so we will be continually tempted to come down and start serving in our own power for our own gain. Satan has a vast arsenal of strategies to woo us from the crucified life and sabotage our service.

BARRIERS TO SELF-SURRENDER AND SERVICE

1. Pride

We cannot help build God's kingdom while carrying a hidden agenda to build ourselves. We may seem productive on the outside, but our spirit on the inside will be churning with a desire to be recognized and promoted. To combat pride we must confess and renounce these cravings. We must also choose not only to serve Christ but to become *a servant of Christ*. Richard Foster insists there is a vast difference between the two:

> When we choose to serve we are still in charge. We decide whom we will serve and when we will serve. And if we are in charge we will worry a great deal about anyone's stepping on us, i.e. taking charge over us.
>
> But when we choose to be a servant we give up the right to be in charge. There is a great freedom in this. If we voluntarily choose to be a servant we surrender the right to decide who and when we will serve. We become available and vulnerable.[1]

This surrender of rights ties in with the biblical definition of servanthood. The Greek word most commonly used for "servant" is *doulos*, which means "slave." This is a subservient image that may be difficult for us to embrace.

However, Paul had no struggle with the concept. He continually referred to Jesus as his "lord" or *kurios,* meaning "absolute owner." Paul insisted that his salvation was purchased by Jesus' death on the Cross.

As a result, Paul no longer belonged to himself. He had been "bought at a price" (1 Cor. 7:23, NIV). Since all believers have been "purchased with the blood of Christ," may we follow Paul's instructions to live "like slaves of Christ, doing the will of God from [our] heart[s]" (Eph. 6:6, NIV). When we consider ourselves possessed by God, unreservedly at His disposal, we deal a fatal blow to pride. Another snare that impedes holy service is:

2. Fear

Many believers avoid serving because they are afraid of taking risks. They feel ill-equipped and sit back, hoping others will step forward to help. Christians of all ages and spiritual maturity levels, however, need to know they are gifted by God and valued by the Church. Each gift, no matter how seemingly insignificant, should be developed and used for God's glory.

It is never too early to be actively involved in Christ's mission, as evidenced by the first disciples who were sent out to serve before Pentecost. Neill Hamilton describes their on-the-job training: "While the disciples were granted some time to observe and listen, they were soon put into mission themselves as extensions of the ministry of Jesus. This occurred long before they had experienced the maturing enlightenment of the transition to life in the Spirit. Even at an immature stage, they were able to do exorcism and healing."[2]

Inexperience or timidity was no excuse to avoid acts of mercy. Wesley admonished the demure Miss March to "put off the gentlewoman; you bear a higher character. Go and see the poor and sick in their own poor little hovels. Take up your cross, woman."[3]

Another snare that hampers our service is:

3. Perfectionism

While some believers are afraid of serving because of the risks involved, others are more anxious about the results. They put unrealistic pressure on themselves or others to produce tangible results that may not be God's priority. This is one reason Paul reminded the Galatians that "God does not judge by external appearance" (2:6, NIV). He does not care about the product of our service as much as the status of our heart in the process of serving. Our efforts to please Him must be matched by an ongoing desire to be like Him.

Susan Muto contends "a competitive spirit, a clever tongue, an analytical mind may place one in the so-called winner's circle" but holy service requires other qualities.

> When we are too pressured, too rushed, too concentrated on our task, too eager to keep things under control and make everything work perfectly, we lose ourselves, we lose our peace, we lose our center. By contrast, it is only when we work from that still and silent center, integrated around the Lord, that we can produce well and respond fully to the people he wants us to touch. It helps a great deal if we can maintain our sense of humor, including the ability to laugh at ourselves and not take things too seriously.[4]

The greatest fulfillment comes when every task is performed in dialogue with the Holy Spirit. He teaches us not to fear failure or idolize success.

He also guards us from the snare of self-pity.

4. Self-pity

Jesus warned His disciples, "In this world you will have trouble" (John 16:33, NIV). The question is, How do we respond to trouble? Do we "take heart," as Jesus suggests, or do we allow our struggles to perpetually rob us of joy and a motivation to serve? Sometimes we can become so absorbed with our pain that there is no interest in reaching out to others suffering alongside us.

Prolonged illness, the loss of a loved one, a broken marriage, unemployment, rejection, or dashed dreams take their toll on our emotions and our health. The natural incli-nation is to withdraw and feel sorry for ourselves. Even Je-sus withdrew whenever He needed personal renewal. In time, however, Jesus always stepped back into the main-stream. He had work to do, a world to redeem, and limited time in which to do it. As God's servants, we also have work to do. Our ministry may be postponed for a while as we squarely address our loss, but it is not meant to be dis-carded indefinitely.

The best counselors for the bereaved are often those who are on the same journey. While trying to organize a support group for grieving believers in our church, I real-ized our widows and widowers did not need psychologi-cal help as much as they needed each other. The loss of sleep, appetites, energy, and even their hair were all a part of the grieving process.

If we truly believe "that in *all* things God works for the good of those who love him" (Rom. 8:28, NIV, empha-sis added), our toughest trials can become beneficial. Suf-fering is not meant to be wasted. It can tenderize our hearts to really feel the aches of others. We may not have all the answers, but we can still come alongside and "com-fort those . . . with the comfort we ourselves have received from God" (2 Cor. 1:4, NIV).

Sometimes all it takes to serve is a Kleenex, as illus-trated by the story of a little girl who came home from a neighbor's house where her little friend had died. "Why did you go?" questioned her father. "To comfort her moth-er," said the child. "What could you do to comfort her?" "I climbed into her lap and cried with her."

Have you ever noticed that crises and peoples' needs often fail to fit into our schedules? That is why the Holy Spirit must also protect us from the snare of inflexibility.

5. Inflexibility

It is difficult to accept interruptions as providential opportunities from God. We often see impromptu needs as threats to our routine. We, like Martha, can be so caught up in a frenzy to fulfill our personal desires that God cannot get through to us to use us. We need to remain open to His surprises.

Enter Archie.

He is an elderly neighbor with the uncanny ability to time his trips to the trash bin with the moment my car enters the driveway. As I get out and shut the car door, I often hear the crash of the garbage can lid. That signals a long conversation is imminent. And I am trapped. After an exhausting day, I am in no mood to talk. I just want to slip into my apartment and be left alone. Yet every time I ask myself, "What would Jesus do?" I am compelled to stop and offer Archie my full attention.

Archie's wife has multiple sclerosis. His life revolves around caring for her. Thus, he has few friends or opportunities to get out and enjoy himself.

One particular afternoon Archie approached me with a puzzled look on his face. "I've been wondering," he muttered. "Why do you take time out to talk to me? Nobody else does."

I paused and marveled at the incredible open door to share Jesus with my old friend. I told Arch, "I talk to you because I care about you. Jesus cares about you too."

After a long conversation about God's love, Archie tearfully admitted. "I've been caring for my wife all alone. It's time I invited God to help me."

There are hurting, searching people such as Archie all around us. And they are watching. They see what we do and the spirit in which we do it. And, in time, most of them can tell if our motives are pure.

That's why we must continually ask ourselves not only what am I doing for God, but **why and for whom am I doing it?** We need to stop regularly to pray with the Psalmist, "Search me, O God, and know my heart; test me and know my anxious thoughts. See if there is any offensive way in me, and lead me in the way everlasting" (Ps.

139:23-24, NIV). Then may we listen inwardly for God's answer. He may reveal to us thoughts and actions when our motives have been less than pure. Pride, fear, perfectionism, or any other snare that has prevented us from being self-surrendered servants must be yielded to the Cross. We must confess any snare and then place ourselves at God's disposal. He and He alone must guide what we do. And He and He alone must receive the glory.

> **If the mainspring of your service is love for Jesus, you can serve men although they treat you as a door-mat.**
> —Oswald Chambers
> *My Utmost for His Highest*

A holy servant displays a singleminded devotion to God. Observe the courage and sacrifice of missionaries such as Elizabeth Cole. She spent years as a nurse in an African leper colony. An American visitor once observed her cleaning the wounds of a leper and said, "I wouldn't do that for a million dollars!"

Miss Cole replied, "I wouldn't either—not for a million dollars, but I would for Christ."[5]

When our focus is to honor God, *all* service, seen or unseen, paid or unpaid, becomes a love offering for God. As Paul told the Corinthians "we are to God the aroma of Christ" (2 Cor. 2:15, NIV). The more available and pliable we are, the more fragrant our witness "for both the saved and unsaved around us."

GOD IS OUR RESOURCE FOR HOLY SERVICE

A holy servant consistently depends on God. Even Jesus never served apart from His Father's direction. Throughout His redemptive mission, Jesus referred to the Father as the following:

His sustainer. "My food is to do the will of him who sent me and to finish his work" (John 4:34, NIV).

His example. "The Son can do nothing by himself; he can do only what he sees his Father doing" (John 5:19, NIV). "For I did not speak of my own accord, but the Father who sent me commanded me what to say and how to say it" (12:49, NIV).

His teacher. "My teaching is not my own. It comes from him who sent me" (John 7:16, NIV).

His glorifier. "If I glorify myself, my glory means nothing. My Father, whom you claim as your God, is the one who glorifies me" (John 8:54, NIV).

Whether Jesus was preaching to the masses, challenging the Pharisees, healing the sick, or raising the dead, He claimed to do exactly what the Father had commanded Him (John 14:31). He never "did His own thing." And in order for our service to have redemptive value, God must be our source as well.

1. God Is Our Source of Direction

I have learned the hard way that God has pledged His support only to that which He has commanded us to do. When we step beyond His call and say yes to every service opportunity that comes our way, we set ourselves up for frustration, guilt, and exhaustion. Overextended servants need to heed the advice of Samuel Rutherford: "There is but a certain quantity of spiritual force in any man. Spread it over a broad surface, the stream is shallow and languid; narrow the channel and it becomes a driving force."[6]

God's direction can help us focus our energies on important things. The insight is ours for the asking. So is God's timing.

2. God Is Our Source for Timing

When we walk in step with the Holy Spirit, God's timing for ministry will be our timing. Sometimes the Spirit bids us to wait, pray, and prepare before stepping out to serve. He often uses these waiting times to build our character and faith for future challenges. For instance, Moses was not called to deliver the Israelites until the Hebrew prince had spent 40 years in the Midian desert. Likewise, Paul's ministry to the Gentiles was postponed until the converted Pharisee had spent at least three years in the Arabian desert.

If you want to serve but are waiting for the opportunity, do not panic. Some of God's most devoted servants have lingered before launching their ministry. Follow their example and use your waiting season to reflect and vitalize your relationship with God. Also, be ready, because the Holy Spirit may call you into active duty at a moment's notice.

I will never forget the night I was awakened by the Spirit to write my father a letter about the joys and eternal benefits of inviting Jesus to be one's personal Savior. I even wrote out a personalized "sinner's prayer" for Dad to recite when he made a decision for Christ.

Little did I know that two days after giving Dad the letter, he would be admitted into the hospital with sharp pains in his left side. Those pains were symptoms of a fast-spreading cancer that took his life within one month!

Two days before his passing, Dad reread my letter and gave his heart to God. His conversion was confirmed to me when I walked into his bedroom. Dad was gazing at the ceiling with his arms upstretched. Although weak, he cheerfully whispered, "I'm ready to go home now. Will you go with me?"

I tearfully assured him, "Yes, Dad. You go on ahead with Jesus. I'll catch up with you later."

When God wants something done, He seeks out servants who are willing to rely on His direction, His timing, and His strength.

3. God Is Our Source for Power

The disciples had the gifts and three years of training with Jesus to preach, teach, heal, and cast out demons. It took Pentecost, however, to empower them to use their gifts with a love and conviction that ultimately changed the world. Being filled with the Holy Spirit, they received power to overcome any rivalry between themselves and any prejudice toward others. They also received power to withstand suffering and keep serving in the toughest of circumstances.

It is God's power that enabled Mary Brown to turn her convalescent home into a mission field. Like most senior adults, she first balked at moving into what she called an "ol' fogy home." She didn't want to leave her apartment, but crippling arthritis left her no choice. After much prayer, she surrendered her independence and entered the home. Through the power of the Holy Spirit, Mary began to focus on the needs of those around her. She recited psalms of love to residents without families. She sang hymns of peace to doctors who raced in and out on breakneck schedules. And she wrote encouraging notes to nurses aides who were fed up with screaming seniors and soiled sheets.

> **Far be it from me to glory
> except in the cross of our
> Lord Jesus Christ, by which
> the world has been crucified
> to me, and I to the world**
> (Gal. 6:14, RSV).

God's power rested on Mary because she pleaded with Him to help her make the most of her predicament. When we genuinely seek God's help, our witness can be infused with similar strength.

Jubilation is another privilege of our inheritance.

4. God Is Our Source for Joy

Jesus came so that His joy would be in us and that our joy would be complete (see John 15:11). Service without Christ's joy often becomes drudgery for those who perform it *and* for those who receive it.

Observe the exuberance of 72 disciples when they successfully completed their first tour of service for the King-dom (Luke 10:1-24). Luke records they "returned with joy" (v. 17). Even Jesus shared their excitement and "was full of joy through the Holy Spirit" (v. 21, NIV). He cautioned them, however, not to rejoice because of what they had done but because of what God had done for them. Consid-ering all that God has done, is doing, and will do for us, may our service bear the fruit of Christ's joy.

Helen Keller wisely contended, "True joy is not at-tained through self-gratifications, but through fidelity to a worthy purpose."[7] Ours is the most worthy purpose of all. As Christians we are called to be "the light of the world" (Matt. 5:14). Jesus compels us to "let [our] light shine be-fore men, that they may see [our] good deeds and praise [our] Father in heaven" (v. 16, NIV).

As partakers of Christ's holy and joyful nature we are called to serve others in a spirit that attracts people to the Father. May we not forget that whenever we serve, God's honor is at stake. And in an era when the integrity of His Church has been blemished by divisions, scandals, and lawsuits, our ministry and motives must be above re-proach.

▶ For Personal Action and Reflection ◀

1. Does My Service Need Servicing?

Before stepping out to serve, stop and ask yourself . . .

A. Am I the surrendered servant God is calling me to be? Available? Willing to tackle any task for God's glory?

B. Am I still in control, determining who, when, and where I serve? Or am I humbly dependent on God's direction, timing, power, and joy to follow through?

C. Are there any "Archies" in my life, unbelievers who are closely observing my witness? If so, is my service attracting them to God? As we will see in the next chapter, what we do for others must be accompanied by Christlike love for them.

2. Bible Study

A. Read Phil. 1:12-26.
B. Note the ways in which Paul practiced selfless service.
C. Memorize Gal. 6:14.

3. Hymn of Commitment

Make the hymn "O Master, Let Me Walk with Thee" a part of your devotions. Make the first verse your prayer.

> *O Master, let me walk with Thee*
> *In lowly paths of service free.*
> *Tell me Thy secret; help me bear*
> *The strain of toil, the fret of care.*
>
> —Washington Gladden

4. A Prayer of Self-surrender

O Lord Jesus,
I give thee my body,
my soul,
my substance,
my fame,
my friends,
my liberty,
and my life:
dispose of me and of all that is mine,
as it seems best to thee.

I am now not mine, but thine:
therefore claim me as thy right,
keep me as thy charge,
and love me as thy child.

Fight for me when I am assaulted,
heal me when I am wounded,
and revive me when I am destroyed.[8]

Holiness is not a private possession granted to select souls but a universal call issued to each of us . . . It is loving God with our whole being and radiating that love in every dimension of life and world.

—Susan Muto
Pathways of Spiritual Living

18

Lord, Intensify My Love for Others

"Where are my toenail clippers?"

Dorothea's belligerent cries rang through the halls of the convalescent home. As I approached her room, a nurse's aide cautioned me, "Enter at your own risk! She's 'raisin' Cain' again. Good luck!"

The warning came just in time. When I walked in the door I was pelted with a barrage of curse words and a flying bedpan! After scrambling out to the hallway, I realized I needed more than luck to reenter Dorothea's room. I needed God's grace—and lots of it!

Dorothea was 72 years old, blind, bedridden, and angry with God and just about everyone else. Throughout her adult life she had learned how to manipulate people to get the attention and the storebought sweets she craved. I was one of many Christians who regularly visited her with a bag of Twinkies, a prayer for her salvation, and continual counsel about her attitude.

This day, however, I didn't feel like praying for her. I was sick of her bitterness and told God so.

"Jesus, I need a break. And if You want me to visit Dorothea, some changes have to take place. First, change this cranky woman's disposition. Then, change my judgmental spirit to see her the way You do. May I remember that 'what I do for one of the least of these, I am doing for you.' You are worthy of my best, so for your glory, I want to offer my best to Dorothea."

After praying and a few deep breaths I reentered the room. Immediately I noticed part one of my prayer had not been answered. Dorothea was as angry as ever. Yet, as I crawled under her bed to look for her clippers, something blessed happened. It seemed as if God's holy presence transformed the room from a war zone into a peaceful sanctuary. Both of us felt it, or should I say, felt Him. Within seconds I stopped fretting and actually began to enjoy Dorothea's company. She, in turn, stopped screaming and, for the first time ever, apologized. Together we laughed and sang old hymns until nightfall. And as I prayed for her and began to leave, Dorothea smiled and whispered, "God's here, isn't He?"

"Yes, dear," I concurred.

"I'm so glad the *both* of you dropped by today."

"Me too," I nodded. "I promise we'll come again."

From that time on, each visit with Dorothea became a divine encounter. Prayer changed my view of service and of people. Indeed, every time I gazed into Dorothea's cloudy eyes and embraced her frail body, I felt as if I was ministering to Jesus himself. She was "one of the least of these" placed into my life to love unconditionally. Regardless of her moods or her response to my care, Dorothea was created in the image of God and merited my undivided attention.

Dorothea taught me that God not only wants us to serve others but wants us to truly **love those we serve.** This was one of Paul's main hopes for the Thessalonians.

He was proud of their service, but he was also elated that "the love every one of you has for each other is increasing" (2 Thess. 1:3, NIV). This is God's wish for us. If we allow Him, He will intensify our love to **see Christ in others** and to **share Christ with others.** These hurting brothers and sisters deserve the same care and respect that we would offer our Savior. What we do for them becomes our love offering to Him.

Pray to Have the Eyes of Christ

Jesus was never too preoccupied with His mission to ignore hurting people. Mark records that Jesus preached from sunup to sundown, yet He could not pass up the opportunity to heal a begging leper (1:41). In the midst of pushing crowds Jesus noticed a despised tax collector and called him (2:14); He felt the tug of a bleeding woman and restored her (5:34). He saw a dead child and raised her (v. 41), and saw the minute offering of a widow and praised her (12:43).

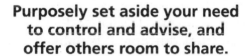

Purposely set aside your need to control and advise, and offer others room to share.

Most of the people Jesus helped were not friends or relatives. They were strangers of all different backgrounds, ages, and afflictions. Still, each one captured His attention and concern.

Strangers may capture our attention, but they rarely evoke enough concern to compel us to service. One reason is that in today's world—with riots, robberies, and drive-by shootings—we are leery of strangers. Why should we try to help someone who may turn around, pull out a gun, and rob us? Television crime coverage has taught us that it is best to lock our doors, hide our valuables, and not get involved.

While it is wise to be careful, may our caution not slip into callousness. Jesus will not work through servants whose eyes are dimmed by indifference.

"PREGNANT, HOMELESS, HUNGRY"—Those were the words printed on a sign held by a young woman on the corner of a busy Pasadena, Calif., intersection. Although it was rush hour, many drivers slowed down to get a second glimpse of the woman. Some of them were Christians who admitted they were led to pray for her. Still, no one stopped. So she waited—and waited. After several hours, someone finally pulled over to help. He was Will Anderson, who happened to be driving through town on his way to a conference.

After a brief discussion, Will found out the woman was 26 years old, eight months pregnant, and without food, a home, or adequate clothing. He called Pasadena First Church of the Nazarene for help. From that point on, the woman received housing, maternity clothing, food, and love from a variety of new Christian friends. She also received assistance to give birth to a healthy baby girl eight days later. After her child was adopted by a Christian couple, the young woman returned to Pasadena to receive counseling for drug addiction. It is unlikely she will forget those who sacrificially assisted her in her desperate hour of need. Among them was a busy man who took time out to stop and look beyond her sign into her soul.

We need Christlike compassion to pay more attention to needy strangers as well as those with whom we interact every day. We can work beside people for years and never really know them.

Everyone in the KNBC newsroom thought he or she knew Andy. He was a well-respected newswriter, addicted to sports and classic Corvettes. Unfortunately, most did not know that Andy was depressed. He was so distraught that, one Friday afternoon, he left work and shot himself. His suicide came as a complete shock. The hundreds who attended Andy's service could not mask their grief. Anchorman Jess Marlow stirred everyone when he tearfully asked, "What's wrong with us? Are we blind? Andy came in day after day and we never bothered to notice he was hurting. We are so busy looking for news that we have forgotten how to look at each other!"

The only way we can be effective servants is to take a closer look at the people around us. May Jesus give us eyes to see a loved one who needs a little extra encouragement. Or may we notice the shy visitor who has slipped into church needing a hug or an invitation to lunch.

PRAY TO HAVE THE EARS OF CHRIST

"Just as love to God begins with listening to His Word, so the beginning of love for the brethren is learning to listen to them."[1] When I enter a conversation with someone in distress I try to remember the example of Mother Teresa, who for years roamed the streets of Calcutta to offer care and dignity to the dying. Each suffering saint received her complete attention. "Every person is Christ for me, and since there is only one Jesus, that person is the only person in the world for me at that moment."[2]

To be good listeners means that we create space within our hearts to receive the joys and cares of others. We purposely set aside our need to talk, to control and advise, and offer others room to share. Rather than assuming people can learn from us, may we posture our minds to learn from them. The more we hear, the more we will understand and know how to respond.

Serving should involve taking the time to hear others, to understand who they really are and what has led them to their present situation. This is the authentic receptivity displayed by Pastor Lee when he introduced me to Christ. I was the reporter assigned to ask him questions about his son's captivity in Iran. Following every interview, he spent time gently inquiring about my life, my profession, and eventually my faith (or lack thereof). Any pressure or preaching would have destroyed the moment. Instead, I felt his unconditional acceptance and a genuine concern for my well-being.

Henri Nouwen describes this kind of a good listener as a "hospitable host." He asserts, "Really honest receptivity means inviting the stranger into our world on his or her terms, not on ours. When we say, 'You can be my guest if you believe what I believe, think the way I think, and behave as I do,' we offer love under a condition or for a price. This leads easily to exploitation, making hospitality into a business."[3]

Hospitable listening does not just automatically happen. It comes from a conscious effort to slow down, put aside our agendas, look into the eyes of others, and pay close attention to what they have to say. Before entering a hospital room to minister to patients, I have learned the value of slowing my pace, praying, and preparing my heart to "take in" their fears, hurts, and hopes. And as I listen, God enlarges my capacity to care.

PRAY TO HAVE THE HEART OF CHRIST

The same mercy that moved Jesus to feed 5,000 hungry followers, to happily embrace giggling children, and to agonize over Jerusalem as a protective hen "gathering her chicks under her wings" is available to God's servants. The closer we are to Jesus, the more our hearts will feel what others feel and will hurt when they hurt.

Matthew Fox contends this Chrislike compassion "is not knowing *about* the suffering and pain of others. It is, in some way, knowing that pain, entering into it, sharing it and tasting it in so far as possible."[4]

Serving with the heart of Christ makes us genuine empathizers with our aching friends. We are to be more than sympathizers who observe pain from afar with an attitude of condescension. If there is one thing hurting people do not need, it is sympathetic clichés such as "I know just how you feel," or "Keep your chin up, kid." Rather, they need servants who will come close and relive to some extent the same pain.

Five-year-old Matthew Taylor and 45-year-old Jay Roth are "blood brothers." They are not bonded by traditional family ties, but by a life-threatening disease and a life-giving sacrifice.

It all began during a costume party in kindergarten, when Matthew suddenly collapsed on the classroom floor. His teacher was alarmed, not so much by the fall, but by his prolonged wailing after the fall.

> **O Father of mercies, grant that I may look on the defects of my neighbor as if they were my own, that I may conceal and be grieved for them; and that making Thy love to us, O blessed Jesus, the pattern of my love to them, I may above all things endeavor to promote their eternal welfare.**
> —John Wesley
> John Wesley's Prayer Manual

A series of tests later revealed Matthew was suffering from acute leukemia. His only hope of survival was a bone marrow transplant, far too strenuous for the boy's weakening body. Matthew needed more blood platelets to build up strength for the transplant. Unfortunately, none of his relatives proved to be suitable donors.

That's when Jay entered the story. Matthew's teacher was a Nazarene pastor's wife who shared the little boy's desperate plight with her church in Newhall, Calif., one Sunday morning. While the congregation prayed, Jay received a distinct impression from God to step forward to help.

In that one instant, all former worries about losing his prestigious bank job and the hassles of moving his family across country disappeared. And even if the platelet-extracting procedure required extra commuter time and tedious hours of lying still in a hospital lounge chair, the sacrifice seemed small compared to the need. All that mattered was that a five-year-old was dying and Jay's platelet-rich blood could possibly save him.

Twice a week for several months Jay made the long trek to UCLA Medical Center to offer up his platelets for a sick child he had never met. By the time Jay and Matthew were introduced, the boy's stamina was strong enough for the bone marrow transplant.

Today, Matthew's cancer is in remission, and he has entered the first grade. His family, amazed by a Christian's generosity and witness, has made several visits to Jay's Nazarene church. And when any thanks or honor come to Jay, he quickly steers all praise to Jesus, who offered His own body and blood to redeem the world.

Jess Moody expressed it so well: "Anybody can salve his conscience by an occasional foray into knitting for the spastic home. Did you ever take a real trip down inside the broken heart of a friend? To feel the sob of the soul— the raw, red crucible of emotional agony? To have this become almost as much yours as that of your soul-crushed neighbor? Then, to sit down with him—and silently weep? This is the beginning of compassion."[5]

A Christlike heart breaks over sin while embracing the sinner. Holy servants need to be channels of God's forgiving love. To do that, we must first recognize that we also have sinned and fallen short of God's glory. Our zeal for their cure must be matched by nonjudgmental care.

My own judgmentalism surfaced one night during a television interview with a pastor whose evangelical church voted to extend membership to homosexuals. Using several scriptures, I valiantly grilled the pastor for his liberal views about the gay life-style. I was feeling a little smug until the program ended. Jenny, a studio worker and dear friend, ambled up to me in tears and whispered, "I guess I wouldn't be welcome in your church."

I was shocked by Jenny's admission. And I was ashamed of my self-righteous spirit that effectively closed the door for any meaningful communication with my hurting friend. Jesus calls us to love others. We are to offer Christ to them, even if we cannot approve of their values or actions. And if we are led by the Spirit to confront them about their behavior, may our words be tempered with love. May we follow the example of our Lord, whose compassion knew no limits.

PRAY TO HAVE THE HANDS OF CHRIST

Jesus understood the value of showing affection. Many of his healings were performed with a gentle touch. Leprous sores, blind eyes, deaf ears, and mute tongues were all cured by His holy hands. His touch imparted hope to strangers and peace to His disciples. After falling face-down with fear on the Mount of Transfiguration, Peter, James, and John were helped up by Jesus. He "came and touched them" and offered them words of comfort (Matt. 17:7, NIV).

> **You . . . have been taught by God
> to love one another; and indeed
> you do love all the brethren . . .
> But we exhort you, brethren,
> to do so more and more**
> (1 Thess. 4:9-11, RSV).

As we serve, our hands can also be tender tools of God's love. A genuine handshake or sweet embrace can communicate a variety of Christlike feelings such as affirmation, care, and trust. Jack and Judy Balswick insist that no one outgrows the need to be held, cuddled, or caressed.

People need to receive overt expressions of love from the time they are born until the day they die. Studies on infant deprivation suggest that babies who do not receive expressions of love will be unable to receive or express love during their entire lifetime.[6]

Research shows that many young women who lacked fatherly affection in their childhood are apt to seek the love they lacked through sexual promiscuity.[7] And many boys who experience aloofness from their parents while growing up are conditioned to later withhold affection to their wives and children.[8]

Love grows in a home and church where people are not afraid to touch. However, we always need the Holy Spirit's guidance to determine when and what signs of affection are appropriate. With the right sensitivity, our hands can convey volumes of forgiving and healing grace.

Many residents in convalescent homes are starving for physical affection. In some homes, senior adults are jostled in and out of bed, force-fed, and strapped in wheelchairs lining the hallways. They crave the touch of a caring visitor. And though they may not see or hear very well, they can feel the gentle strokes of a friend. The same is true for seriously ill patients in hospitals. Sometimes the best relief for fear and pain is our hand calmly clasping theirs.

PRAY TO HAVE THE VOICE OF CHRIST

To serve others with the love of Jesus, we must follow His example by choosing and using our words wisely. Jesus was a peerless communicator. He suited His words to each occasion and each audience. Sometimes He spoke as a prophet forecasting doom for those who failed to obey God. At other times He spoke as a counselor drawing out the innermost thoughts of His followers. We see Him as a teacher mystifying the multitudes with His parables or just as a friend conversing at a dinner table. He was a clever debater who could level His attackers with devastating accuracy, or a caring physician who could raise the sick with divine authority.

His words packed a punch because Jesus knew who He was and what He was called to do. He was the Son of

God, sent by the Father (John 4:34), loved by the Father (10:17), and called to please the Father (5:30).

When we consider that we are coheirs with Christ, called, loved, and commissioned by Him, our words also can have a powerful impact. The name of Jesus and the Holy Spirit's unction sharpens our words to penetrate the hardest of hearts and softens our words to lift the lowest of hearts.

Proverbs makes it clear, "Death and life are in the power of the tongue" (18:21, KJV). The old childhood rhyme "Sticks and stones may break my bones, but words can't ever hurt me" simply does not hold true. Words *can* hurt, and, as the proverb implies, they can be lethal.

We should consider Paul's charge to the Thessalonians to "encourage one another and build each other up" (1 Thess. 5:11, NIV). Whatever we say should affirm others rather than tear them down. Our conversations should promote harmony rather than division. While serving, may we "always try to be kind to each other and to everyone else" (v. 15, NIV).

May our loving service resemble that of the first Christians, who caused Roman officials to sit up and take notice. The next time we step out to serve, we should consider this observation from Aristides to the Roman emperor Hadrian: "They [Christians] love one another. They never fail to help widows; they save orphans from those who would hurt them. If they have something they give freely to the man who has nothing; if they see a stranger, they take him home, and are happy, as though he were a real brother. They don't consider themselves brothers in the usual sense, but brothers instead through the Spirit, in God."[9]

▶ For Personal Reflection and Action ◀

1. **Think about how you respond to people such as:**

   A. Dorothea who was disabled, cranky, and desperately needing love.

B. The young, homeless, pregnant woman who stood on a busy corner seeking help.

C. Andy, the coworker who appeared competent on the outside, but inwardly was contemplating suicide.

D. Jenny, the lesbian who wanted to know if she'd be scorned or welcomed by my church.

E. Think of the people God has placed in your life. Think of the times you have or have not really noticed them. Then ask God to increase your capacity to see, hear, feel, touch, and speak His love to them.

2. Bible Study

A. Reread 1 Thessalonians 1—3. These chapters have been at the heart of previous studies in this book. But a quick review will be profitable.

B. Study Eph. 4:1-16. Record in your journal notes about the spirit, tone, and structure of Christian service.

C. Submit Eph. 4:15 to *lectio divina,* that is, an exercise of *spiritual reading.* Let the focal point be "speaking the truth in love."

3. Journal Exercise

A. After you have read this chapter and studied 1 Thessalonians 1—3 and Eph. 4:1-16, write in your journal your responses to this quotation from Dietrich Bonhoeffer: "Jesus is looking for help, for He cannot do the work alone. Who will come forward to help Him?" *(The Cost of Discipleship).*

B. Sing and meditate on these two hymns: "Take My Life, and Let It Be Consecrated" (Hymn 455 in *Sing to the Lord*) and "Where Cross the Crowded Ways of Life" (Hymn 537 in *Sing to the Lord*). Note in your journal insights or blessings these songs bring.

> The church is a training facility or staging area to launch members into mission, a M*A*S*H* unit to return them to service when they are wounded in the line of duty, a rest area in which they can catch the breath of the Spirit when fatigue in mission sets in.
> —Neill Hamilton
> *Maturing in the Christian Life*

19

Finding My Places of Service

Concerned friends told Los Angeles Mission worker Rich Verbal it couldn't be done—it shouldn't be done. Taking a group of homeless men from skid row on a camping trip to the mountains was beyond the call of duty, even dangerous. How would this motley troop fare in the wilderness? How would they get along with each other?

Rich wasn't sure. All he knew was that the idea was born in prayer and that if God wanted him to follow through, He would provide the grace and supplies to do it. As Rich saw it, the benefits of such a journey far outweighed the barriers. Camping under the stars would show the former gang members that there was more to the sky than smog, more to the earth's floor than concrete, and more to the animal kingdom than rats and pigeons. With faith, borrowed tents, and fishing poles, he took the van load of young men from six different cultures on a four-day adventure.

The results were phenomenal. Cultural differences

disappeared as the men fished, rode bikes, sang, and testified around the camp fire. Ray, an ex-convict who was forced to grow up quickly on the streets, summed up the group's appreciation: "For the first time ever, I was able to release the child bottled up inside of me."

That release came as the result of their leader's obedience. Rich wasn't a psychologist or an ordained elder, just a willing servant with a deep love for God and a genuine concern for his homeless brothers.

As we have seen in the last two chapters, holy service evolves from this kind of surrendered life-style. When our motives are pure and our hearts are filled with Christlike love, we can impact our homes, churches, neighborhoods, workplaces, and world. In this chapter we will examine service opportunities awaiting us when we offer up all we have and do for God's glory.

> **Let us go forth, tis Christ commands,**
> **let us make haste away.**
> **We offer to Christ our heart and**
> **hands,**
> **we work for Christ today.**
> —Charles Wesley

The Bible makes it clear that service is not a means of salvation but the natural product of our holy hearts. And as we grow in Christ, there is a natural "rhythm or flow from inspiration to incarnation, from prayer to participation, from contemplation to action."[1]

William Barclay contends: "It is a fact that every time a man feels a noble impulse without taking action, he becomes less likely ever to take action. In a sense it is true to say that a man has no right to feel sympathy unless he at least tries to put that sympathy into action."[2]

To help fulfill our call to holy service, God has equipped us with one or more spiritual gifts. These are unique abilities the Holy Spirit gives us us after our conversion that enable us to build up and encourage others. The great majority of gifts are mentioned in Rom. 12:6-8; 1 Cor. 12:4-11; and Eph. 4:11. Every believer has at least one of these gifts and will be held accountable to use it.

If you have any doubt, take another look at Jesus' parable of the talents. He described three stewards who received different quantities of capital. Their responsiblity was to use their resource to make more money. Two of the three succeeded and doubled their money. When the day of accounting came, they were called "good and faithful servants." The other steward failed to recognize the potential of the resource he had. He did nothing with his capital and was judged a "wicked, lazy servant" (Matt. 25:26, NIV; see vv. 14-30).

From this story we learn that whatever resources we have received from God cannot be hidden but must be used to accomplish the Master's purpose. Many Christians are accomplishing God's purpose without being able to describe their specific gifts. There is biblical ground, however, for knowing and developing these gifts. Paul urges, "Now about spiritual gifts, brothers, I do not want you to be ignorant" (1 Cor. 12:1, NIV). One reason we should not be ignorant is that understanding and using our gifts will help the church to function. When "each separate part works as it should, the whole body grows" (Eph. 4:16, TEV).

The church body will grow, however, only as each part (Christian) relies on the Holy Spirit for gifting and direction. We cannot casually browse through gifts like a shopping list and pick whichever one sounds good. Nor are we free to choose no gift and opt out of Christian service. Without self-giving service, all the other spiritual formation activities treated in this book are reduced to mere shadow boxing.

SERVICE AS A SPIRITUAL DISCIPLINE IN THE HOME

The first place we should exercise our gifts to serve is in our home with those who are closest to us. Richard Foster contends, "The dictum for the household should be 'Let each of you look not only to his own interests, but also to the interests of others' (Phil. 2:4, RSV). Freely and graciously the members of the family [should] make allowance for each other."[3]

Before racing out to fulfill their call as holy servants in the world, husbands and wives should first express God's love to each other. They need to

Serve each other permission to discuss misunderstandings, reveal hurt feelings, air frustrations, and ask difficult questions.

Serve each other freedom to make and recover from mistakes.

Serve each other understanding not only to tolerate but to celebrate the differences in their character and personality traits. When we quit passing moral judgment and learn more about our separate temperments, we open the door for workable compromise.

Serve each other encouragement to be all God wants us to be and do what God calls us to do. Men should be encouraged to break out of the macho, independent mold shaped by society and place their lives under God's control. At the same time, women need encouragement to develop inner security that comes from pleasing God. A husband's openness and imput can help his wife overcome cultural pressures either to stay home or to venture into the marketplace. Couples should also

Serve each other time. Solid relationships require regular breaks built into our busy schedules for "dates" to enjoy each other's company. Finally, it is essential for a husband and wife to

Serve each other authentic love. First, love needs to be offered verbally. It is important to tell each other regularly, "I love you." We need to back up our words with affectionate action. Whatever is said and done in love will build a mate's self-esteem and have a powerful impact on the entire family.

Raising children in a healthy, secure home requires years of sacrificial service. Henri Nouwen reminds us:

Children are not properties to own and rule over, but gifts to cherish and care for. Our children are our most important guests, who enter into our home, ask for careful attention, stay for a while and then leave to follow their own way. . . . What parents can offer is a home, a place that is receptive but also has the safe boundaries within which their children can discover what is helpful and what is harmful. There their children can ask questions without fear and can experiment with life without taking the risk of rejection.[4]

Parents need to serve their children with fervent prayers to protect them, wisdom to guide them, fair discipline to train them, and opportunities to instill responsibility. Assigned chores let children know they are contributing members of the family.

> **There should be less talk; a preaching point is not a meeting point. What do you do then? Take a broom and clean someone's house. That says enough.**
> —Mother Teresa of Calcutta

The foremost concern in raising children should be to introduce them to a dynamic relationship with Jesus. Neill Hamilton claims this often is not the case: "I am afraid that most parish parents are content with their parenting if their children move smoothly to acquire the manners and education necessary for upward mobility. Parents are better at equipping their children to grow up achievers than they are at equipping them to grow up Christian."[5]

So much of what children feel about God and the Church is developed by watching their parents. My roommate, for instance, grew up in a home where hurting, lonely people were welcomed and housed for as long as they needed. Throughout her high school years Dana watched her parents offer hospitality to teenagers and young adults craving love and stability. This invaluable service has influenced Dana's Christian walk. Following her parent's example, she frequently turns our apartment into a hospice for new believers who need love and nurturing.

As singles, we, too, are called to love and serve those God has placed in our lives, especially friends and housemates. Simple expressions of care such as praying for each other, listening to each other's experiences, fulfilling household chores, paying bills on time, and respecting each other's possessions and privacy create an atmosphere of hospitality.

Unbelievers may be able to serve each other with the same consideration, but it takes a holy life **to consistently want** to serve others. Our surrender coupled with God's grace can transform a home into a haven of safety where all are affirmed and encouraged to grow in Christ.

SERVICE AS A SPIRITUAL DISCIPLINE IN THE CHURCH

The church committed to holy service is made up of Christians who have an intense love and feeling of responsibility for each other. Believers are bonded by

1. A Call to Community

Christians should have a compelling desire to give themselves away for the common good. Charles R. Swindoll claims this corporate identity in Christ turns believers from "marbles" to "grapes." "Every congregation . . . can choose to be a bag of marbles, single units that don't affect each other except in collision. Or . . . a bag of grapes. The juices begin to mingle, and there is no way to extricate yourselves if you tried. Each is a part of all. Part of the fragrance . . . [and] sometimes we 'grapes' really bleed and hurt."[6]

The joy of being a part of a church with a serving heart is that no one bleeds and hurts alone. Regardless of our trials or triumphs, someone will come alongside and share the experience with us.

Ask Miriam. She was 76 years old when she asked Christ into her heart. Her first Christmas as child of the

King, however, almost changed her mind. First, she caught a nasty cold. Second, she was fired from her job. Then her dogs broke down the fence in her front yard at about the same time her wall heater died. As she shivered in her frigid little house, Miriam heard several gunshots. Running outside, she found one of her dogs lying dead on the front lawn. The other dog was injured.

Miriam was devastated and cried out, "What's with You, God? Don't You love me anymore?" She screamed so loud that she almost didn't hear the phone ring. The call was from one of her new friends from church who felt led by God to phone Miriam "to see if everything was all right." Miriam was stunned. How did her friend know she needed help?

The friend listened and immediately came over with firewood to heat Miriam's house and an extra hand to take the wounded dog to the veterinarian. The next day an electrician from the church came to repair her heater while a handyman from the church put up the frontyard fence. A few days later a Sunday School class took up an offering to help Miriam pay her bills. They came to her door singing carols, bearing a big basket of food and a decorated Christmas tree, complete with lights and ornaments. "God loves you, Miriam," one of the carolers exclaimed.

"I know," she admitted. "I now really know."

The spontaneous care from other believers prompted Miriam to stay in the church and become involved in the pantry ministry for the homeless.

2. A Call to Responsibility

If holiness is to be expressed through good works, then the church is called to equip, motivate, and send *all* believers into service. Hear the rally cry of pastor and lay ministry leader James Garlow: "Contrary to popular opinion Christianity is not a spectator sport. Every believer is a minister! Everyone is involved."[7]

As we have seen in earlier chapters, this involvement

was extensively promoted by John Wesley, who trained 653 lay preachers during his half century of active ministry. The early Methodist system gave ample room for laypersons to serve as class leaders, band leaders, stewards, visitors of the sick, schoolmasters, and housekeepers.

Thomas Gillespie contends this sweeping lay revolution will continue today, but "only if the 'nonclergy' are willing to move up, if the 'clergy' are willing to move over, and if all God's people are willing to move out."[8]

As we minister together not only as servants but as true friends of Jesus and each other, we can fulfill Paul's command to "do good to all people, especially to those who belong to the family of believers" (Gal. 6:10, NIV).

At the church I attend, members are heeding the commission to "carry each other's burdens" (Gal. 6:2, NIV) in a variety of ways. Teens visit shut-ins. Shut-ins write encouragement cards to teens. Young couples renovate the homes of members in financial trouble. Older couples "adopt" young families by frequently contacting them and interceding for them. Mechanics assist widows with car problems. Accountants counsel single parents surviving on limited incomes. And prayer groups of all ages regularly meet to lift the church's praises and petitions to the throne. The call to holy servants extends beyond where we live and where we worship to where we work. When Christians walk on the job they should be thinking about more than making money, impressing the boss, or surviving until the weekend. Regardless of where we work, ultimately we are to serve Christ and the people for whom He died.

Paul makes it clear that "whatever you do, work at it with all your heart, as working for the Lord, not for men, since you know that you will receive an inheritance from the Lord as a reward. It is the Lord Christ you are serving" (Col. 3:23-24, NIV). In other words, our ultimate boss is Jesus.

The songs of our spiritual ancestors, the early Wesleyans, should be ours. This song was titled "On Their Going to Work."

Let us go forth, Tis Christ commands,
Let us make haste away.
We offer to Christ our hearts and hands,
We work for Christ today.[9]

—Charles Wesley

SERVICE AS A SPIRITUAL DISCIPLINE IN THE WORLD

The more God's servants heed His upward call to holiness, the more concerned and involved we must be with His idolatrous world. Our journey is not to retreat to a stained-glass ghetto to wait patiently and passively for the consummation of the Kingdom. Rather we must live and work for the sake of the Kingdom now. We are partners with Christ to promote His righteousness and justice throughout creation. Our global mission is threefold.

1. *Witnessing the Gospel:* We are called to preach and model the good news to all people.

2. *Charity:* We are called to offer relief to the needy and oppressed.

3. *Social Action:* We are called to hold social structures accountable to Kingdom principles.

1. Servants Are Called to Witness for the Gospel

Holy servants are called to live and proclaim the gospel so as to win people to a personal faith in Jesus Christ. It is not enough to introduce them to Jesus; we must disciple them to submit their lives to His grace, Lordship, and mission.

Often the toughest mission field is witnessing to those we know and love the most. I shared my frustrations with former Nazarene General Superintendent Dr. Edward Lawlor one day. He advised me to find a pen and paper to record his answer. When I returned, he offered three ways to witness to my lost loved ones. "Number one: kindness and understanding. Number two: kindness and understanding. Number three: kindness and understanding." His advice reshaped my approach to sharing Christ with others.

We also need to be involved in the church's corporate mission to proclaim Christ to our neighboring community and world. I am reminded of the redemptive work by several of my friends who are following in the footsteps of John Wesley and Phineas Bresee.

—Ed sponsors a neighborhood weekly Bible study that has attracted a growing number of believers and nonbelievers near his home.

—Sandy consistently invites unsaved friends to church. Her ministry has helped win more than 15 people to Christ in the last two years.

—Willie has struggled with cancer for years. Still, between chemo treatments, she offers Bibles and blankets to teenage runaways on the streets of Hollywood.

—Wes is a retired judge who enjoys interaction with people of different cultures on Work and Witness projects.

—John heads up a young couples missionary chapter that is devoted to assisting home mission churches all over the Los Angeles Basin.

2. Servants Are Called to Aid the Poor

Throughout the Bible we see God taking special interest in the needy and inviting us to do the same. John F. Alexander observes, "The fatherless, widows, and foreigners each have about forty verses that command justice for them. God wants to make it very clear that in a special sense He is the protector of these weak ones. Strangers are to be treated nearly the same as Jews, and woe to people who take advantage of orphans or widows."[10] Prov. 14:31 reminds us: "He who oppresses the poor shows contempt for their Maker" (NIV). At the same time, "He who is kind to the poor lends to the Lord" (Prov. 19:17, NIV).

The best way to help the poor is to identify with them. That's what Jesus did. Paul tells us that "though he was rich, yet for your sakes he became poor" (2 Cor. 8:9, NIV). He was born in a lowly stable. His parents were too poor to bring the normal offering for purification (Luke 2:24).

During His public ministry He didn't have a home of His own (Matt. 8:20). He even sent out His disciples in poverty (Luke 9:3; 10:4).

So what does this mean to you and me? It means that we are to follow Christ's example by choosing to be with the poor. May we listen to them, learn from them, and express Christlike mercy to them.

John Wesley contended that there was no split between personal salvation and social engagement. He and his reformers worked tirelessly for the spiritual and material welfare of those victimized by industrialization. Wesley spread scriptural holiness and reformed the nation by establishing social services such as orphanages, poor houses, food and clothes pantries, a free medical clinic, a "lying in" hospital for unwed mothers, and boarding schools for children otherwise destined for work in the sweatshops and mines.

> **Let us not grow weary in well-doing, for in due season we shall reap, if we do not lose heart. So then . . . let us do good to all men**
> (Gal. 6:9, RSV).

On top of that, Wesley urged Christians to give away all but "the plain necessaries of life—that is plain, wholesome food, clean clothes and enough to carry on one's business."[11] He lived what he preached. Sales of his books often earned him £1,400 annually, but he spent only £30 pounds on himself. The rest he gave away. He always wore inexpensive clothes and dined on simple food.[12]

The call to simplicity was echoed by Nazarene leader Phineas Bresee, who wanted houses of worship "plain and cheap" so that "everything would say welcome to the poor." Early Nazarene churches were encouraged to spread holy fire through preaching and loving service to the needy. The social ministries of the church included Rest Cottage, a rescue home for unwed mothers in Pilot Point, Tex.; a storefront rescue mission in downtown Los Angeles; and an orphanage in Bethany, Okla. The heritage of holy service lives on today in a variety of compassionate ministries to assist those whose lives have been devastated by relatively recent tragedies such as the riots in Los Angeles and Hurricane Andrew in Florida and Lousiana. Churches throughout the United States have united in prayer and projects to rebuild demolished homes, churches, and businesses. And to address international needs, Christians have distributed offerings or hard work to bring food to starving families in Africa and medical relief to victims of the nuclear plant explosion in Chernobyl, Russia.

Regardless of our incomes, *all* believers are called to conform our spending and working habits with a sensitivity to the needs of others. We should stop buying frivolous things in order to generously give more to God's causes. Parents should model biblical stewardship to their children. Richard Foster writes, "Neither Jesus nor any of the apostles confined giving to the tithe—they went beyond it. In all their teachings, generosity and sacrifice loom large. This is true whether we are looking at the poor widow giving her mite or Barnabas giving a parcel of land to the early church."[13]

3. Servants Are Called to Social Action

As holy servants we are called to promote God's peace in a world infected by greed, permissiveness, and selfishness. With Jesus as our model and the Spirit as our enabler—

We can confront injustice. We should commend our government, schools, and health organizations whenever they act to preserve biblical standards. We should support leaders or assume leadership ourselves to initiate change for the public good. It is our right and responsiblity to stand up for the rights of the unborn, the elderly, the mentally retarded, and others who are unable to fend for themselves. We can do this through prayer, vigorous nonviolent demonstration, and personal intervention into the lives of suffering people. May we as individuals and together as the Body of Christ *intentionally* seek those shunned by society to offer them God's healing grace and hope.

Some servants may feel led to expose injustice by taking part in civil disobedience. Before we challenge civil authority, however, Christians must make sure they are walking in the authority, power, and love of the Holy Spirit.

We can confront immorality. Sin has distorted our world's view of sexuality. May we as God's servants exemplify good morals and speak out against pornography and promiscuous behavior so often promoted by the media. Parents need to teach and model for their children what the Bible says about sexuality and proper relationships.

We also need to hold the media accountable for its publications and programming that so often condone immoral behavior. We should voice our displeasure by writing well-researched, concise letters to publishers, television producers, and sponsors. Our opinions can make a difference.

And we can confront pollution. It's time to become better stewards of God's creation. Our homes and churches should explore creative ways to conserve more and consume less. Christ's servants should take the lead in recycling to cut down waste. We should also help to clean up our communities for future generations.

Before moving on, stop and think about your spiritual journey as God's servant. Recall the people and needs He has placed on your path and your response to them. While heeding the upward call, have you received and imparted God's grace to your family, to your church, to friends at work, neighbors across the street and strangers you've met? Have you used the spiritual gifts, possessions, and personality God has given you to improve the quality of life around you? Are you consumed by a passion to *be* good news as well as *share* the Good News?

Lord, may we consistently poise our lives for a fresh infill-ing of the Holy Spirit to see, cry, and care for the needs of Your hurting world.

▶ For Personal Reflection and Action ◀

1. Bible Study

    A. Read Ephesians 5—6
    B. List what these chapters say about
    Christian service in the church
    Christian service in the home
    Christian service in the world

2. Harvesting the Best Ideas in Chap. 19

    A. Review the chapter and note the items in it that echo your own strong convictions

    B. Identify the examples or ideas in this chapter that make you uncomfortable, make you feel guilt or conviction.

    C. If you could have a 15-minute conversation with the author, what topics would you raise?

3. Narrowing the Gap

    A. In your journal, draw a simple diagram that compares on a scale of 1 to 10 where you *are* and where you would *like to be* in regard to Christian service.

    B. What steps can you take *this week* to narrow the gap between where you *are* and where you would *like to be?*

EPILOGUE

UNGUESSED GLORIES
AND UNFATHOMED DEPTHS

You have come to the end of this book but not to the end of your spiritual journey. Unguessed glories and unfathomed depths of His grace lie before you, waiting to be discovered.

You will discover them as you give yourself to the pursuit of Christlikeness. As noted early in this work, the goal of spiritual formation and sanctifying grace is Christlikeness. As E. Stanley Jones once said, "Holiness divorced from Christlikeness is not holiness, but hollowness."

The Bible tells us how we become more like Christ. "And all of us, with unveiled faces, seeing the glory of the Lord as though reflected in a mirror, are being transformed into the same image from one degree of glory to another; for this comes from the Lord, the Spirit" (2 Cor. 3:18).

This verse inspired the first stanza of Charles Wesley's famous hymn "Love Divine All Loves Excelling."

> *Finish then Thy new creation;*
> *Pure and spotless let us be.*
> *Let us see Thy great salvation,*
> *Perfectly restored in Thee:*
> *Changed from glory into glory,*
> *Till in heav'n we take our place,*
> *Till we cast our crowns before Thee,*
> *Lost in wonder, love, and praise.*

The team has written this book to give guidance in understanding the fundamental patterns of holiness. We have tried to provide a comprehensive understanding of the overall patterns of spiritual formation with the guidance of the Word of God. We recognize that we have not touched on every subject.

For example, the role of music in the devotional life probably deserves more emphasis. Also, suffering as a spiritual discipline could have been explored with profit. After all, when God decided to redeem the world, He chose to do it through suffering. As Christ's followers, our suffering, though it may appear wasted, has some redemptive contribution in the world. Suffering, therefore, has meaning. Not that one should seek suffering for its own sake. But we should know that all suffering consecrated to Christ has redemptive value.

Further, we recognize that we have not written exhaustively on the topics we have addressed. Yet we pray and dare to hope that it has helped produce in your heart a hunger to dedicate yourself to following the upward call of God to Christlike living. We pray that, even at this moment, your heart opens upward and sings this prayer to our gracious God:

"Finish then thy new creation."

NOTES

Preface

1. Frank Whaling, *John and Charles Wesley: Selected Writings and Hymns,* in *The Classics of Western Spirituality* (New York: Paulist Press, 1981), 64.

Chapter 2

1. Susan Howatch, *Scandalous Risks* (New York: Alfred A. Knopf, 1990), 255.

2. Steve Turner, "Lean, Green, and Meaningless," *Christianity Today* 34:13 (Sept. 24, 1990), 27.

3. Ibid.

4. Walter Brueggemann, *Finally Comes the Poet* (Minneapolis: Fortress Press, 1989), 30.

5. H. Ray Dunning, *Grace, Faith, and Holiness* (Kansas City: Beacon Hill Press of Kansas City, 1988), 278-83.

6. *The Works of John Wesley,* 3rd ed. (Kansas City: Beacon Hill Press of Kansas City, 1979 reprint of 1872 edition), 6:67-68.

7. Dunning, *Grace, Faith, and Holiness,* 275.

8. Mildred Wynkoop, *A Theology of Love* (Kansas City: Beacon Hill Press of Kansas City, 1972), 164.

9. Ibid., 154.

Chaper 3

1. Dunning, *Grace Faith, and Holiness,* 478.

2. Robin Maas, *Crucified Love: The Practice of Christian Perfection* (Nashville: Abingdon Press, 1989), 105.

3. Ibid., 21.

4. Maas, "Wesleyan Spirituality," in *Spiritual Traditions for the Contemporary Church,* ed. Robin Maas and Gabriel O'Donnell (Nashville: Abingdon Press, 1990), 311-12.

5. Ibid., 311.

Introduction to Part II

1. Dallas Willard, *The Spirit of the Disciplines: Understanding How God Changes Lives* (San Francisco: Harper and Row, 1988), 137.

2. *The Works of John Wesley* 5:187-88.

Chapter 4

1. Annie Dillard, *Teaching a Stone to Talk* (San Francisco: Harper and Row, 1982), 40.
2. R. A. Torrey, quoted by Daniel J. Lehman in "Evangelizing Evangelicals," *Christian Century* 105:30 (October 19, 1988), 917.
3. William Temple, *The Hope of a New World* (New York: Macmillan, 1942), 30.
4. Evelyn Underhill, *Worship* (London: Nisbet and Co., 1936), 72.
5. In German, the words *Volkswerk, Volksdienst,* and *Gottesdienst* all combine the concept of obedient service owed with reference to the one to whom that obedience is owed—whether society or God.
6. Robert E. Webber, *Worship Is a Verb* (Nashville: Abbott-Martyn, 1992), 16-18.
7. John E. Burkhart, *Worship* (Philadelphia: Westminster Press, 1982), 17.
8. Oscar Cullmann, *Early Christian Worship* (London: SCM Press, 1953), 29.
9. Rob Staples, *Outward Sign and Inward Grace* (Kansas City: Beacon Hill Press of Kansas City, 1991), 99.
10. Maria Harris, *Fashion Me a People* (Louisville, Ky.: John Knox Press, 1989), 77.
11. Staples, *Outward Sign and Inward Grace,* 100.
12. Walter Brueggemann, *Israel's Praise: Doxology Against Idolatry and Ideology* (Minneapolis: Fortress Press, 1988), 139.
13. Ibid., 133.
14. Brueggemann, "Praise and the Psalms," *The Hymn: A Journal of Congregational Song* 43:4 (October 1992), 18.
15. Cited by Clyde E. Fant, *Preaching for Today* (New York: Harper and Row, 1975), 22.
16. Richard Lischer, *A Theology of Preaching* (Nashville: Abingdon, 1981), 74.
17. Webber, *Worship Is a Verb,* 11.
18. Ibid., 79.
19. Staples, *Outward Sign and Inward Grace,* 106.
20. Ibid., 108.
21. Harris, *Fashion Me a People,* 77.

Chapter 5

1. *The Works of John Wesley* 5:188.
2. Ibid., 201.
3. Ibid., 192.
4. Ibid., 194.
5. Ibid., 3.
6. Ibid. 14:252.
7. Ibid., 253.
8. John Wesley, *Explanatory Notes upon the New Testament* (Kansas City: Beacon Hill Press of Kansas City, 1981 reprint), vol. 2, notes on 2 Tim. 3:16.

9. *The Works of John Wesley* 14:253.
10. Ibid.
11. Eugene H. Peterson, *Working the Angles: The Shape of Pastoral Integrity* (Grand Rapids: William B. Eerdmans Publishing Co., 1987), 61.
12. Ibid., 80.
13. Walter Ong, *The Presence of the Word* (New Haven, Conn.: Yale University Press, 1967), 19.
14. M. Robert Mulholland, Jr., *Shaped by the Word: The Power of Scripture in Spiritual Formation* (Nashville: Upper Room, 1985), 58.
15. *The Works of John Wesley* 14:253.
16. Ibid.
17. Dietrich Bonhoeffer, *The Way to Freedom: Letters, Lectures, and Notes 1935-1939* from the *Collected Works of Dietrich Bonhoeffer*, ed. Edwin H. Robertson, trans. Edwin H. Robertson and John Bowden (London: Collins, 1966), 2:59.
18. Ibid.
19. Mulholland, *Shaped by the Word*, 110.
20. Ibid.
21. Ibid., 111.
22. Walter Brueggemann, *Interpretation and Obedience* (Minneapolis: Fortress Press, 1991).
23. *The Works of John Wesley* 14:253.

Chapter 6

1. Susan Muto, *Pathways of Spiritual Living* (Petersham, Mass.: St. Bede's Publishing, 1984), 115.
2. John Wesley, *The Letters of the Rev. John Wesley, A.M.*, ed. John Telford (London: Epworth Press, 1960), 5:212.
3. Ibid., 275-76.
4. Maxie Dunnam, *The Workbook of Intercessory Prayer* (Nashville: Upper Room, 1979), 17.
5. Kenneth Leech, *True Prayer* (San Francisco: Harper and Row, 1980), 59.
6. Ibid., 60.
7. Author's paraphrase of 1 John 1:7.
8. Macarius the Egyptian, "Homilies," *A Christian Library*, ed. John Wesley (London: T. Blanchard, 1819), 1:81.
9. Ibid., 97.
10. Ibid., 110.
11. Ibid., 100.
12. Albert E. Day, *Discipline and Discovery* (Nashville: Disciplined Order of Christ, 1961), 89.
13. John Wesley, "The Repentance of Believers," *Sermons on Several Occasions* (London: Wesleyan-Methodist Book Room, n.d.), 185.
14. Wesley, "Our Lord's Sermon on the Mount," Discourse III in *Sermons*, 326.
15. Bob and Michael W. Benson, *Disciplines for the Inner Life* (Waco, Tex.: Word Books, 1985), 337.

16. See *Weavings* 1:1 (September/October 1986), 36-38.

17. Muto, *Pathways of Spiritual Living,* 121, 123.

18. Quoted by Stephen J. Harper in "The Devotional Life of John Wesley, 1703-1738," Ph.D. diss., Duke University, 2:403. This is from Harper's transcription of Wesley's handwritten prayer manual.

19. John Wesley, "John Wesley's Covenant Service," in *Wesley Hymns* (Kansas City: Lillenas Publishing Co., 1982), A-4.

Chapter 7

1. Willard, *The Spirit of the Disciplines,* 161.

2. Henri J. Nouwen, *Out of Solitude* (Notre Dame, Ind.: Ave Maria Press, 1974), 20.

3. Thomas R. Kelly, *A Testament of Devotion* (New York: Harper and Row, 1941), 102.

4. Muto, *Pathways of Spiritual Living,* 77.

5. Ibid., 78.

6. Henry J. Nouwen, *The Way of the Heart* (Minneapolis: Winston/Seabury Press, 1981), 12.

7. Anthony Pavadano, *Dawn Without Darkness* (New York: Doubleday and Co. 1972), 123.

8. Muto, *Pathways of Spiritual Living,* 57-58.

9. Selected from "A Practice-of-Silence Test," in Wayne Oates, *Nurturing Silence in a Noisy Heart* (Garden City, N.Y.: Doubleday and Co., 1979), 112-13.

10. John Wesley, *The Sermon on the Mount, John Wesley's Fifty-Three Sermons,* ed. Edward H. Sugden (Nashville: Abingdon Press, 1983) 7:334.

11. Ibid., 344.

12. Ibid., 342.

13. James C. Fenhagen, *Ministry and Solitude: The Ministry of Laity and Clergy in Church and Society* (New York: Seabury, 1981), 68.

14. Les L. Steele, *On the Way* (Grand Rapids: Baker Book House, 1990), 33.

Chapter 8

1. Robin Maas and Gabriel O'Donnell, *Spiritual Traditions for the Contemporary Church* (Nashville: Abingdon Press, 1990), 46.

2. Ibid., 47.

3. Muto, *Pathways of Spiritual Living,* 74.

4. Maas and O'Donnell *Spiritual Traditions for the Contemporary Church,* 48.

5. Susan Muto, *Meditation in Motion* (Garden City, N.Y.: Image Books, 1986), 26.

6. J. I. Packer, *Knowing God* (Downers Grove, Ill.: InterVarsity Press, 1973), 117.

7. Morton Kelsey, *The Other Side of Silence* (Ramsey, N.J: Paulist Press, 1976), 36.

8. Ibid., 37.
9. Ibid., 39.

Chapter 9

1. Ross Snyder, Introduction to Robert Wood, *A Thirty-Day Experiment in Prayer* (Nashville: Upper Room, 1978), 7.
2. Wood, *A Thirty-Day Experiment in Prayer*, 14.
3. Muto, *Pathways of Spiritual Living*, 111.

Chapter 10

1. Annie Dillard, *Pilgrim at Tinker Creek* (Toronto: Bantam Books, 1974), 149.
2. Willard, *The Spirit of the Disciplines*, 139.
3. Some valuable resources for gaining insight into the way in which Myers-Briggs personality indicator affects spiritual development can be found in the following resources: Steve Harper, *Embrace the Spirit* (Wheaton, Ill.: Victor Books, 1987); W. Harold Grant, Magdala Thompson, and Thomas E. Clarke, *From Image to Likeness* (New York: Paulist Press, 1983); Reginald Johnson, *Celebrate, My Soul: Discover the Potential of Your God-given Personality* (Wheaton, Ill.: Victor Books, 1988); and M. Robert Mulholland, Jr., *Invitation to a Journey: A Road Map for Spiritual Formation* (Downers Grove, Ill.: InterVarsity Press, 1993).

Chapter 11

1. Wally Fahrer, "We Are Committed to Each Other," *Gospel Herald* (Feb. 18, 1992), 2.
2. Holland N. McTyeire, *A History of Methodism* (Nashville: Publishing House of the M.E. Church, South, 1904), 204.
3. *The Works of John Wesley* 1:416.
4. Ibid. 3:144.
5. Steven Harper, *Embrace the Spirit* (Wheaton, Ill.: Scripture Press/Victor Books, 1987), 90-91.
6. *The Works of John Wesley* 8:269.
7. Fahrer, *Gospel Herald*, 2.
8. *The Letters of the Rev. John Wesley, A.M.* 8:158.

Chapter 12

1. John W. Drakeford, *People to People Therapy* (San Francisco: Harper and Row, 1978), 21.
2. *The Letters of the Reverend John Wesley, A.M.* 2:115.
3. From an article in *Zion's Herald* (Boston: Nov. 21, 1825) 3:1. It was designated as a reprint from an earlier edition of Wesley's *Arminian Magazine*.
4. Ibid.
5. Ibid.
6. Ibid.
7. Ibid.
8. *The Works of John Wesley* 8:270.

Chapter 13

1. *The Works of John Wesley* 8:258.
2. Charles L. Goodell, *The Drillmaster of Methodism: Principles and Methods for the Class Leader and Pastor* (New York: Eaton and Mains, 1902), 239.
3. *The Works of John Wesley* 8:272-73.
4. G. Byron Deshler, *The Power of the Personal Group* (Nashville: Tidings, n.d.), 6.
5. Ibid., 15.
6. *The Works of John Wesley* 8:259-60.
7. *The Letters of Rev. John Wesley, A.M.* 7:91.

Chapter 14

1. Translation by F. F. Bruce in *World Biblical Commentary*, ed. David A. Hubbard and Glenn W. Barker (Waco, Tex.: Word Books, 1982), 28.
2. Allan Jones, *Exploring Spiritual Direction* (New York: Seabury Press, 1982), 77-79.
3. Kenneth Leech, *Soul Friend* (San Francisco: Harper and Row, 1977), 88-89.
4. *The Letters of John Wesley* 2:187.
5. Ibid. 7:187.
6. Ibid. 5:93.
7. Ibid. 7:24-25.
8. Ibid., 45-46.
9. Ibid. 6:261-63.
10. Ibid. 8:84.
11. Ibid. 6:144. (For a comprehensive study of Wesley as spiritual guide to Ann Bolton, see "John Wesley, Spiritual Director: Spiritual Guidance in Wesley's Letters" by Wesley Tracy, *Wesleyan Theological Journal* [Spring 1988], 148-59.)
12. Carl Jung, *Modern Man in Search of a Soul*, quoted by Edward C. Sellner in *Mentoring, the Ministry of Spiritual Kinship* (Notre Dame, Ind.: Ave Maria Press, 1990), 28.
13. Sharon Parks, *The Critical Years: The Young Adult Search for a Faith to Live By* (San Francisco: Harper and Row, 1986), 88.
14. Quoted by Edward C. Sellner in *Mentoring: the Ministry of Spiritual Kinship*, 61.
15. *The Letters of John Wesley* 3:94-95.
16. Sondra Higgins Matthaei, "Faith Mentoring in the Faith Community" (Unpublished Ph.D. dissertation, Claremont School of Theology, 1986), 9.
17. Alice Frazer Evans, Robert A. Evans, and William Bean Kennedy, *Pedagogies for the Non-Poor* (Maryknoll, N.Y.: Orbis Books, 1987), 283. Quoted by Matthaei in "Faith Mentoring in the Faith Community," 10.
18. Matthaei, "Faith Mentoring in the Faith Community," 71.

19. Quoted by Matthaei, "Faith Mentoring in the Faith Community," 12.
20. Sellner, *Mentoring: the Ministry of Spiritual Kinship*, 76.
21. Ibid., 23.
22. Matthaei, "Faith Mentoring in the Faith Community," 18.
23. Ibid., 37.
24. *The Letters of John Wesley* 7:174.
25. Ibid. 3:103.
26. Matthaei, "Faith Mentoring in the Faith Community," 41.
27. *The Letters of John Wesley* 5:62.
28. Ibid. 7:56.
29. Ibid., 59.
30. Matthaei, "Faith Mentoring in the Faith Community," 14.

Chapter 15

1. Bruce, *Word Biblical Commentary*.
2. Ibid., 53.
3. *The Letters of John Wesley* 5:258.
4. Ibid., 87.
5. Bruce, *Word Biblical Commentary*, 59.
6. Ibid., 10.
7. Ibid., 34.
8. Matthaei, "Faith Mentoring in the Faith Community," 62.
9. Laurent Daloz, *Effective Teaching and Mentoring* (San Francisco: Jossey-Bass, 1987), 231.
10. William H. Willimon, "Taking Confirmation out of the Classroom," *Christian Century* 105:9 (March 16, 1988) 271. Cited by Matthaei, "Faith Mentoring in the Faith Community," 60.
11. Cited by Matthaei, "Faith Mentoring in the Faith Community," 61.
12. Bruce, *Word Biblical Commentary*, 28, 65.
13. Ibid., 34.
14. See Matthaei, "Faith Mentoring in the Faith Community," 63-67.
15. Stephen Crane, "A Learned Man" in *Modern American Poetry* (New York: Harcourt Brace & World, 1958), 148.
16. William Myers, *Theological Themes of Youth Ministry* (New York: Pilgrim Press, 1987), 35.
17. Matthaei, "Faith Mentoring in the Faith Community," 66.
18. Bruce, *Word Biblical Commentary*, 70.
19. Ibid., 128.
20. James Fowler, *Becoming Adult, Becoming Christian* (San Francisco: Harper and Row, 1984), 40.
21. Sellner, *Mentoring: the Ministry of Spiritual Kinship*, 77.
22. Daloz, *Effective Teaching and Mentoring*, 19.
23. Christina Downing, *The Goddess: Mythological Images of the Feminine* (New York: Crossroad, 1981), 105, 107. Cited by Matthaei, "Faith Mentoring in the Faith Community," 6.

Chapter 16

1. *Conference Minutes* 1:52, 68, cited by John W. Prince, *Wesley on Religious Education* (New York: Methodist Book Concern, 1926), 134.
2. *Conference Minutes* 1:81, cited by Prince, 135.
3. John Wesley, "On Family Religion," *The Works of John Wesley* 7:79.
4. Ibid., 80.
5. "A Thought on the Manner of Educating Children," *The Works of John Wesley* 13:476.
6. Ibid. 7:81.
7. Ibid.
8. *Conference Minutes* 1:4, cited by Prince, 133. Also see *The Works of John Wesley* 5:194.
9. John Wesley, *John Wesley's Prayers*, ed. Frederick C. Gill (New York: Abingdon Press, 1951), 59, 63.
10. *Wesley Hymns*, A-4.
11. "The Devotional Life of John Wesley," 2:538.
12. *John Wesley's Prayers*, 103.

Chapter 17

1. Richard Foster, *Celebration of Discipline* (San Francisco: Harper and Row, 1978), 115.
2. Neill Hamilton, *Maturing in the Christian Life* (Philadelphia: Geneva Press, 1984), 127-28.
3. *The Letters of the Rev. John Wesley, A.M.* 6:153.
4. Muto, *Pathways of Spiritual Living*, 173.
5. *Missionary Featured at the Church of the Nazarene*, biographical sketch on flier prepared by the Department of World Missions, Church of the Nazarene, Kansas City, Cory Abke, "Interview: President Don Owens," Accent on MidAmerica Nazarene College, Summer 1988, 12.
6. Quoted by Amy Carmichael in *Kohila* (Washington: Christian Literature Crusade, n.d.), 139.
7. Quoted by James S. Hewett in *Illustrations Unlimited* (Wheaton, Ill.: Tyndale House, 1988), 280.
8. "The Devotional Life of John Wesley, 1703-1738," 2:355.

Chapter 18

1. Dietrich Bonhoeffer, *Life Together* (New York: Harper and Row, 1952), 99.
2. Mother Teresa of Calcutta, quoted by Malcolm Muggeridge in *Something Beautiful for God* (San Francisco: Harper and Row, 1971), 118.
3. Henri J. M. Nouwen, *Reaching Out* (Garden City, N.Y.: Doubleday, 1975), 69.
4. Matthew Fox, *A Spirituality Named Compassion* (Minneapolis: Winston Press, 1971), 21.
5. Jess Moody, *Quote-Unquote*, ed. Lloyd Cory (Wheaton, Ill.: Victor Books, 1977), 66.
6. Jack and Judith Balswick, *The Family, A Christian Perspective on the Contemporary Home* (Grand Rapids: Baker Book House, 1991), 201.

7. Dan Benson, *The Total Man* (Wheaton, Ill.: Tyndale House Publishers, 1977), 178.

8. Ross Campbell, *How to Really Love Your Child* (Wheaton, Ill.: SB Publications, Victor Books, 1977), 47-51.

9. *Apology* 15, in *The Anti-Nicene Father*, ed. Allan Menzies, (New York: Charles Scribner's Sons, 1926).

Chapter 19

1. Susan Muto, *Pathways of Spiritual Living*, 31. For further study on the rhythms of contemplation and service, see Muto's book *Renewed at Each Awakening: The Formative Power of Sacred Words* (Denville, N.J.: Dimension Books, 1979).

2. William Barclay, *The Letters of James and Peter Daily Study Bible Series* (Philadelphia: Westminster Press, 1958), 76.

3. Foster, *Celebration of Discipline*, 107.

4. Nouwen, *Reaching Out*, 58-59.

5. Hamilton, *Maturing in the Christian Life*, 167.

6. Charles R. Swindoll, *Dropping Your Guard: The Value of Open Relationships* (Waco, Tex.: Word Books, 1983), 178.

7. James L. Garlow, *Partners in Ministry* (Kansas City: Beacon Hill Press of Kansas City, 1981), 21.

8. Thomas Gillespie, "The Laity in Biblical Perspective," *The New Laity*, ed. Ralph D. Bucy (Waco, Tex.: Word Books, 1978), 32.

9. Quoted by David Michael Henderson in *John Wesley's Instructional Groups* (Unpublished Ph.D. dissertation, Indiana University, 1980), 124.

10. John F. Alexander, "The Bible and the Other Side," *The Other Side* 11:5 (September-October 1975), 57.

11. See *The Works of John Wesley* 5:361-77.

12. J. Wesley Bready, *England: Before and After Wesley* (London: Hodder and Stoughton, n.d.), 238.

13. Richard Foster, *Money, Sex & Power* (San Francisco: Harper and Row, 1985), 73.

A 13-session leader's guide for group study is available. Order from your local bookstore or contact Beacon Hill Press of Kansas City
P.O. Box 419527
Kansas City, MO 64141.